OSUNYAMEYE

OSUNYAMEYE

NOTHING IS IMPOSSIBLE WITH GOD

HILDA MANYO DICKSON

When baptised, you named me Hilda. I doubt you knew it meant war or battle.

Further down the road, you called me a go-getter then advised I live a life of forgiveness to clear my path for challenges ahead.

I barely understood the context, but I kept pushing. Positivity welled up within and has stayed with me.

To my mum and every fighter who keeps on pushing, I dedicate this to you.

Blessèd, who from years of sorrow,
Bitter days and dim of scope,
Still, can keep the fire of hope
Burning, for a brighter morrow;

Who can keep alive his yearning
For God's help and victory still,
Trusting Him to hold and heal
And raise joy in place of mourning.

Onesi Dominic

TABLE OF CONTENTS

Acknowledgements

When I vowed to write a book, I imagined it would be a breeze. After all, it was my story to tell and mine to write. How wrong I was! I never imagined it would be such a challenging process, but it has also been rewarding. It would have been impossible to achieve this without the ensemble of wonderful people that keep lighting up my path.

To everyone who nudged me on, put in a positive word, criticized the process, and believed in me, I start by thanking you for the part you played. The thought that went into the action you put forward, the impact it made and the joy it brought to my heart are of inestimable value. It matters to me! I say thank you.

To my exceptional husband and all-time boyfriend: thank you so much for cheering me on and taking most chores off me to ensure I focused

i

on my writing goal. To my outstanding children, Innomama, Onohnse and Osaki, thank you for the many parts you played in editing, choosing the cover page and just understanding me when stress loomed. I love you so much.

A special thanks to Singto Saro-Wiwa, my amazing sister-in-law: I made the vow; you took the pilot's seat. I set out to write a specific testimony, but you reminded me I had a rich story and needed to share more. You provided an outline over six years ago, insisted I write a book, not a leaflet. You edited the first draft and still called my proud 25,000-word-count book a pamphlet. I pushed back but yielded to more writing, then more editing, and today we have a book. Thank you!!!

When I started writing, I did not have a book title, but my dear friend Amara Chibundu kept nudging me to continue to write *A Day Called Hope*, the title she gave the book. It had that title for almost a decade before it metamorphosed to *Osunyameye*. Thanks for your inputs and for reading through the various drafts; you have been consistent through it all. You have several books in you, and I look forward to reading them.

To Lois Oni, the gifted confidence coach, Funke Omodele and Ibelema Green: you were my extra pairs of eyes when I needed neutral parties to read through the book, check the flow of thoughts and make inputs. You all painstakingly did so and provided constructive feedback.

Chiomah Momah, Titi Horsfall, Othuke of Masobe books: you're a collection of talented writers. Your tips came in at the tail end but were a necessity to complete the process. Thank you.

Onesi Dominic, my birthday mate: I thought you had abandoned me, but God knew when I needed you most and reserved you for the end. Thank you won't cut it. Just know that I appreciate it all.

To Susan Hughes, the thorough editor, and Rachael Ritchey, who created the breathtaking cover design, I say thank you for your patience and for trusting the process.

To my various prayer communities and partners - Girl Power, Watchers, House of Mary,

Raising Leaders, Taggers: You might not have prayed specifically for this book, but each time we prayed, a burden was lifted, a vision was caught and there was an illumination. Thank you.

Pastor Chris and Yemisi Ugoh: I enjoyed and gleaned from your teachings for over two decades. Even when I imagined the obstacles were insurmountable, you sent me right back to the drawing board. Thank you very much for being outstanding teachers and mentors. I have infused a lot from the teaching that I have applied in my life's journey in this work.

Reserving the very best for last:

To My BIG God: I struggle to find the right words to say thank you. None of this and none of me would have been complete without Your amazing grace. Thank you, Lord, for being my present help always.

Prologue

As a teenager, I had dreams of the strong, beautiful and fulfilled woman I wanted to become, and the path was clear to me. I set academic, personal, spiritual, health and several other goals, all in my head. I started off with a plan to study pharmacy in the university, until I realised that it would be a five-year course, which I considered too long; I just wanted to be done with school and start living out my dreams. So, I came up with the excuse that I detested the smell of chemicals and decided to pursue a four-year course in accounting instead.

My plan was to graduate from the university at the age of 22, get married at 25, have two or maybe three children before turning 30, and voila! I would be ready to focus on all other goals, reach the peak of my career, retire to some exotic place with my husband eventually and just keep loving my dream life. I had it all figured out before I stepped out confidently to accomplish my goals.

When we take the time to map out a strategic plan for the foreseeable future, a false sense of peace can envelop us. But even when we assess risks and make contingency plans to cover all the potential loopholes, dealing with deviations from the plan, while daunting for some, can be an adventure worth exploring. Life's curveballs can be exciting, even when they disrupt our best-laid plans with the unpredictable.

Could you be that young lady or family that started off with a clear plan, as I did?

Could the hiccups have started even before you carried out any of the plans?

Then, more hiccups even as you struggled to grapple with the first?

Could you have waited for some years to have a child or dealt with a sick child?

Have you been heartbroken? Discouraged? Confused?

Have you moved on, or are you still stuck in a state of despair?

While we all long to be able to relate an exciting testimony filled with praise and positivity, I doubt if any of us are really prepared for the inevitable trials which are an inescapable part of life; neither are we ready for the gruelling tests accompanying them. I can say this with certainty: I was not ready, despite the rocky paths I had already encountered. But with the firm and constant knowledge that nothing is impossible with God, our ultimate victory is assured, regardless of whether the outcome is positive or negative from an earthly perspective.

Join me as I share with you my journey into the unpredictable!

CHAPTER ONE

The Beginning

It was a day like any other, in September 1999. As I read the dailies, which I rarely did, I suffered a rude shock. My friend had been killed in the Niger Delta waters by the 'Egbesu' boys, a militant wing of the Ijaw youth council in the South-South region of Nigeria. Could life be that short? Could it end so abruptly with no goodbyes? *We must have a purpose beyond all this*, I thought. *There must be a better plan. God's plan is for good.* I felt there must be more to life than chasing money, fame and

1

shadows, but these ponderings about life's purpose put my typically vibrant, talkative self in a deep reflective mode.

At the time, I was working for a commercial bank in the Trans Amadi axis of Port Harcourt, a town in southern Nigeria. I had never really wanted to be a banker, for I knew that beyond the nice suits, ties and somewhat flashy cars were lives that lacked balance. Working late into the night was typical, rather than the exception, for the operations staff of the bank. We opened to clients at eight in the morning and closed the banking doors at four. Left in the hands of a sporadic internet connection, we then had to see to it that all the day's transactions were captured in the books to ensure that the CABAL, a summary of client cash balances from the previous day, was accurate for the following day if needed for customer transactions when the banking systems were not working optimally. Though technological awareness and advancement was on the rise, this process remained slower than it was intended. We spent between six to eight hours posting transactions after shutting the doors to clients each day.

Ironically, to stay focused and to better manage the rather stressful work conditions, we spent the evenings cracking jokes, struggling to speak the little French we knew and discussing random topics while balancing the books ahead of the next day's cycle. When I learned about my friend's death, I withdrew for a bit from all the hilarity. I just needed some level of calmness to help me organise my space and thoughts.

I lived in a safe and prestigious area of Port Harcourt popularly known as Old GRA (Government Reserved Area). One of my favourite uncles, Bisong, had graciously provided a room that I shared with an old friend from the university. It was nicely tucked away in the service quarters with my uncle's domestic staff. It was our first accommodation as young workers, and we were quite proud of our tidy little room. We entertained close friends often, and they were intrigued whenever they visited our room because we had an open-style wardrobe with shelves that were always as neatly arranged as a showroom.

I recall one day when connectivity at work had been relatively stable, and we had been able to post our transactions online in real time. As a result, I made it home that night in record time. I had barely settled down and still had my work clothes on when two colleagues from work appeared at my door unannounced. One of them, Femi, was a close friend who was very jovial and full of pranks. He had a strange way of being insulting in an amiable manner, such that the recipient rarely ever took offence. His sense of humour was remarkable. Femi and another mutual friend and colleague, Nike, dropped by from time to time, but tonight Femi was accompanied by a colleague I barely knew and hardly ever even spoke to, a handsome young man who joined the bank two months after I did.

I remember his first day at work. His arrival in a red Toyota Corolla had some of us wondering who he was, as new intakes like us commuted with taxis or motorcycles popularly known as 'okada'. A friendly office manager had given him a nickname that suited him so well: 'Oyibo'– not just because he was light-skinned but because he spoke with a somewhat Western accent we popularly referred to as 'phone', which is short for phonetics. In our little gossip corridors, we got to know he had previously worked for one of the many oil and gas companies in Port Harcourt and was not a new intake in the sense we viewed it.

That was all I knew about him, because they immediately assigned him to the auxiliary cash office the bank ran at The Presidential Hotel, one of the big government-owned hotels in Port Harcourt. We had not really had a lot of interactions, as our paths rarely crossed at work. The cash office where he worked had no internet connection at all, so he had to come over to the main office each day to have his entries posted. Even though he spent two to three hours each day in the banking hall, he spent most of his time by the cash counters, while I was always in my corner of the bank in the Funds Transfer unit. We rarely shared more than occasional pleasantries. Now why was he at my house? *Strange*, I thought. Well, there were no rules, so we welcomed all visitors.

We got to talking, and my unasked question came to the fore. He wondered why I had been so quiet for the past couple of days. No chitchat, jokes or loud noises in the banking hall? I had no idea he noticed anything that went on in any other part of the banking hall than the cash and teller section. So, I shared my story of how I lost a friend I considered close. He was not just a friend, but someone I had dated briefly. We had parted ways in February 1999. He retraced his steps after probably trying out another relationship and returned in June of the same year to apologise. He asked for a second chance, which I was not ready to gamble with, and I made that clear. His last request was that I spend his birthday with him in August, and I also turned him down. I often joked that the first seven-day fast I had ever embarked

6

on was because of a man – and he was that man. I had seven prayer points that were all answered. I remember vividly that one of my prayer requests was to be able to forget about that relationship and find the strength to move on. God answered and I was at peace, which was why when he returned there was no going back for me. Now that he was gone forever, I guess it was understandable that my quietness was more reflective than depressive. There was really nothing more obvious than the fleeting nature of life at that time.

That visit was the birth of a new friendship. Oyibo became a wonderful friend of mine. We started talking more often at work. He would check up on me regularly, calling from the cash office where he worked. Whenever he had the chance, he would drop me off at my place on his way home. We really enjoyed each other's company. He was a gentle, God-fearing man who respected boundaries, and I found him genuinely caring. Our friendship was such that I did not feel under any pressure. It was genuine friendship with no strings attached, and that mattered a lot to me. He was in a relationship, and I was not looking for one, so it worked perfectly. We would spend hours talking about random things, analysing issues, strolling, laughing, being happy and, sometimes, deliberating on relationship-related matters. Femi, Nike, and I co-opted Oyibo into some of our local outings, which ranged from stopping at a food seller's place on our way home to eat some roadside meals, to purposely targeting Amala joints (a popular meal eaten in the western part of Nigeria) or going to the amusement park for a day and so much more.

I remember travelling to Lagos for a training, and when I returned, he was waiting at the airport to pick me up. He gave me some fun friendship cards, which I was certain he got from Nik-Nak, a popular superstore then that had a lot of nice cards and cute gifts. As he dropped me off at home, he remembered he had an appointment with his girlfriend and was running very late. I advised him to go right back to Nik-Nak and get an apology card for keeping her waiting, which I am certain he did.

We continued to enjoy this friendship that many could neither explain nor understand. We had a routine of reaching out to each other every morning for a recap of the previous day. This was before GSM phones were introduced. Thuraya phones were the only mobile phones available at that time and were so expensive that only the rich could afford them, so he would reach me through the bank's central line. The secretary to the branch manager manned this line. When Oyibo started getting questioned on why he was always calling, he switched to using strange names each time he got in touch. Sometimes it was Henry, which coincidentally is also his name, and at other times he was Frederick. I always found the names a funny decoy. Now when I think back on it, I really wonder what we perpetually discussed, but it sure had an enjoyable feeling.

One year down the line, Oyibo decided he wanted to try his hand at something different.

Working in a bank had been a last resort for him. He needed to keep busy and earn a living, but his heart was in the oil sector, as he was a trained geologist. Opportunity soon came knocking and he got accepted into the Shell Intensive Training Programme for graduates that offered a diploma. He seized the opportunity to resign from the bank to pursue this course which he hoped would give him an advantage and possibly even earn him immediate employment into any multinational oil and gas company.

This created an instant vacuum. I knew I would miss my friend, but it was all for good, so I wished him well and encouraged him to chase his dreams. He was no longer in a relationship, so there was really nothing keeping him back in Port Harcourt. Off to Warri, Delta State, he went, while I stayed on in Port Harcourt. We continued to be in touch and talked whenever his intensive programme gave him a breather.

Three months later, he visited Port Harcourt without any notice and stopped by to see me. It was a pleasant surprise and a splendid opportunity to catch up on the last three months. Oh, my joy knew no bounds. We hugged each other so tightly that a passerby would assume we had not seen each other for ten years. I was very excited and so was he.

He seemed to have a mission on that visit. He came over to my place with public transport, so it was clear we would not be driving around. We spent a lot of time talking about his new life as a student in Warri and what had gone on in the banking sector since he left. As we settled down to a meal, he suddenly popped an unexpected question. He simply asked if I could wait until he ended the intensive study programme to marry him. That was the last thing on my mind, though we had built a relationship over a season. My answer was not exactly straightforward, but more of a conditional yes, because I needed to do some praying. He handed me a lovely commitment ring, which he had connived with our mutual friend Nike to arrange through her fiancé in London. I wondered how he knew my ring size, and after searching my thoughts, I remembered a thread trick for measuring my fingers which Nike had performed sometime back. The engagement ring would come thereafter, hopefully. I surely did look forward to the future with this fine man!

The friendship had transitioned to a courtship.

CHAPTER TWO

Making Progress

I shared my new status as a commitment ring bearer with my family and close friends while continuing to pray for God's guidance. The first person to get the news that Oyibo had proposed to marry me was my mother.

Phone booths installed by the Nigerian Telecommunications Company (NITEL) could be found in various locations in town. I went to the one nearest to me, somewhere between The Central Bank of Nigeria and State Secretariat in

Port Harcourt. Considering it was a Saturday night, the call centre did not have many people, so it was easy to share the exciting news. I was aware it was just the first step. I struggled with different emotions as my fingers dialled the phone numbers, but my analytical mind kept me busy and focused on reaching my mother. One dial and the call went through! It seemed this news wanted to go out fast. As I waited for my mother to pick up the line, I wondered if Oyibo had shared the news with any of his siblings or close friends. Did anyone who mattered to him know the steps he had taken? I was not too sure, but I felt safe enough to nurse the idea of finalising the process someday.

Finally, someone picked up the line. 'Mum!', I screamed, unable to contain my joy.

***

Now the mini waiting game commenced. He still had roughly nine months to the end of his training. We managed to stay focused for academic reasons, as it was an intensive course which naturally came with some demands, while respecting the physical boundaries we had agreed to. I had an opportunity to visit Oyibo at the study centre twice during his stay and could attest to the fact that it was a place for serious-minded people. He exuded a lot of positive energy, and I was certain he had made the right decision to resign from his job at the bank and start afresh.

Oyibo successfully completed the programme at the end of July 2000 and returned to Port Harcourt. We anxiously awaited the outcome of the placement, as not everyone who went through the programme was retained by the company. Unfortunately, when the placements were published, we were disappointed he did not get his dream job. Regrettably, there was a pause in the scheme of things. All the 'why' questions popped up from all angles. Everyone wondered what went wrong. A tough one, having such a close opportunity that seemed to have slipped through his hands.

Oyibo spent most of his time reading the worn copy of the *Good News Bible* inherited from his late mum, whom he adored so much. He stayed hopeful, putting every effort towards searching for similar jobs in the oil and gas industry. It seemed to be an arduous task, but he did not want us to put our wedding plans on hold. I was always reminded of the Bible verse, Psalm 37:24: 'Though he falls, he shall not be utterly cast down, for the Lord upholds him with his hand'. I did not think it was the right step to take, considering the job quest. I did not want him under any pressure. I advised that we wait a little longer till he got a job, as there was really no hurry, but Oyibo was determined to tick getting married to me off his to-do list.

Coincidentally, I was in the process of getting another accommodation, as my uncle Bisong, who graciously housed me, had been transferred by his company to Benin City, which was in another state. Bisong's colleague took over the house and gave me a quit notice almost immediately, informing me that I would have to vacate the property. I was jolted. What was I going to do, I wondered? I tried to ask for an extension from the new occupant, but the appeal fell on deaf ears. I was caught between getting a new accommodation and having to get married shortly after. What a waste of the much-needed finances. I had looked up a few places and was close to selecting one when Oyibo came up with a different idea. He suggested we rent a bigger apartment, which I could stay alone in until the marriage plans were concluded. I think that was a reinforcement pillar, and it drove the matter home: Oyibo meant business and was ready to get married. I bought into the idea, and that was how I started living all by my lonesome self in a three-bedroom apartment in Rumuomasi, Port Harcourt.

Bold step that was, as Oyibo was bent on using his savings from his previous years of working to carry out the wedding plans. We settled on a convenient time in October to introduce our families to each other. We started with my mum, who lived in Calabar. He came with his mother's older siblings, Uncle Mike and Aunty Gubsie, whom he had lived with in Port Harcourt for six years. Next, we drove four hours to Bendeghe Ekeim.

The family introductions went on without any hitches, and our families fell in love with each other. There were no objections raised. It was a very successful trip, in my opinion. Though Oyibo had no job at the time, he was such a likeable and sincere person that all they could see was the potential and not the present state of things.

The next step was to arrange the traditional marriage rites and then the white wedding. The wedding plans kicked off, and I barely participated in planning any event. The bride's family was required to organise the traditional marriage. My mum had that covered, so I only needed to arrive two days before the event. We had our traditional marriage ceremony on 15 December 2001, in Bendeghe Ekeim. The turnout was impressive. We never imagined that our friends and colleagues would make the road trip. The court wedding was held five days later in Port Harcourt. It was a simple, no-frills occasion.

Oyibo worked closely with Aunty Gubsie, who was an unrivalled event manager, to plan the white wedding. On 5 January 2002, we had a garden wedding at the serene Tevit Homes, in Old GRA Port Harcourt. It would not be out of place to say we had a fully sponsored wedding. We didn't have to take a loan or beg for a dime, because love and support flowed from all sides—family, friends, acquaintances... just name it. We had no cause to touch our savings. We enjoyed a lot of goodwill, and the wedding venue was a sight to behold. Aunty Gubsie reserved a lovely room for us at the venue, where we spent our first night as man and wife. To sum it up, we enjoyed unprecedented favour, and we had a beautiful wedding. I was now officially Mrs. Manyo Hilda Dickson, nee Tangban, wife of Mr. Tobin Kio Kweku Henry Dickson.

***

Many new couples look forward to a great honeymoon after the wedding, but we had more on our minds. It was wedding done, what next? Any job around the corner? We felt it was important to have a little getaway nevertheless, so we travelled to Lagos and spent some time in the house where Tobin spent most of his childhood years, in Dideolu Estate, Ogba. It may not have been the honeymoon of our dreams, but we were content and happy.

A month after the wedding, Tobin got a job in an indigenous oil and gas company in Benin City, Edo State. It was not a well-paid job by any standard; he earned a fourth of what he had been earning before he left the banking industry, but he was determined to cater for our family, and his decision to take up the job earned him my respect. I had mixed feelings, as I had never envisaged starting off married life with my husband living in a different city, but that was my new reality, and I had to face it. Notwithstanding, we were thankful.

In fact, as far as I was concerned it bore truth to the Bible verse that says: 'He who finds a wife finds a good thing and obtains favour from the Lord'. After all, he had been without a job for over six months.

It was a three- to four-hour journey to Benin from Port Harcourt which, though tedious, was better than doing nothing. Besides, remember that my uncle Bisong had moved to Benin, so we had family there too. That and more was enough to keep our gaze upwards.

After the wedding celebrations, the real marriage starts. You begin to realise that things that one probably ignored while courting become more obvious, and the unique differences between persons from diverse backgrounds become glaring. Some negligible, some really a big deal. We had to adapt to each other's culture and language differences, and many things became learning points, such as relational issues and eating and cooking patterns. This was especially true for the woman. I remember the first day I heard him call his aunty, who was more than 25 years older, by her first name. I recall saying to myself in Pidgin English, 'This na real oyinbo'.

Then I realised that I must not get Tobin upset or he might not eat my meals. And sometimes it felt like learning to walk on eggshells was a prerequisite for a peaceful marriage. I even discovered different cooking methods for meals that I had always cooked while growing up, like frying ripe plantain with or without salt, soup with or without tomatoes, and how to dispose of waste and serve food. The list could go on and on. One may have had various ideologies on how to resolve disputes before marriage, but the sooner you move off theoretical fantasy to reality, the better for everyone. Learning to unlearn and relearn was an ongoing concern. As individuals we had our expectations, but we both had to work towards knowing each other better and adapting to the new us.

Things started happening fast. Tobin resigned from the job in Benin after three months. He realised it was not worth all the stress. Thankfully, an opportunity opened up in Port Harcourt at the private banking unit of the same bank where I still worked, this time at a higher level, which he gladly accepted. While working in the same organisation with my spouse had its downsides, we were excited by the prospect of living in the same city. At that point, I was transferred to the cash office where he originally worked; it was necessary to avoid any conflict of interest arising in the course of carrying out our duties.

Soon after Tobin got the job, the rumour mills became active. A few colleagues were aggrieved and wondered why he would resign and come back to a better position. It did not matter that he had returned with a higher level of education. The reaction was understandable, although it further buttressed the fact that one man's gain would most likely result in another's pain. So yes, life is generally not fair.

Thankfully, all that silent rift was short-lived, as he got yet another job which was more aligned to his aspirations a few months later. This time, the role was even farther away, in Lagos, just as I was finally beginning to enjoy the idea of being married and doing things together. So, with the new distance, I found myself on another rollercoaster of emotions. Well, I had to brace up and support his dream, which I could very much relate with. One key reason I pitched my tent in Port Harcourt in the first place was to get an opportunity to work in the oil and gas industry.

***

So, with the wedding over, marriage training ongoing and jobs settled, what next? The life plans began. Man-made plans and God's plan. I remember attending several weddings where the presiding minister declared over the couple that in nine months they would have a child to be christened or dedicated to God. We had even teased once and wondered whether the couples had the same prayer or if it was an imposed prayer. We had the same declaration over our lives during our wedding. We chuckled because we had desired to spend the first year discovering and knowing each other. We would start having kids in the second year to allow us to settle into a schedule. That was our plan.

Growing up, I had really looked forward to the onset of my monthly periods. As a preteen, I believed that would truly make me a big girl. When it eventually started, I wished it never had. I suffered severe period pains clinically known as dysmenorrhoea. It had been a constant factor since puberty, so almost anyone who was in my circle had an idea of what went on every month. While in boarding school, I never missed my monthly visit to the sick bay. I suffered several embarrassing moments. I had a very heavy flow, and the outfits I wore that were not black were easily stained, even when I used multiple layers of sanitary towels. This continued right through to the university.

The pain was nearly unbearable. During my second year in the university I attended classes from home, as getting accommodation on the university campus was not only expensive but difficult. My maternal grandmother spent her last two years before she passed on with us and witnessed me go through so much pain. She shared her experience with me and how she used a drug called codeine to manage her pain. She encouraged me each time and assured me it would be a thing of the past once I started having children.

At some point, I thought I had gathered enough experience in managing dysmenorrhoea and the attendant questions and never imagined the narrative would be different after marriage. Each month the pain returned, people assumed I was pregnant and teased it was the new bride's sickness or morning sickness. I found it very annoying. I lost my sense of humour at such times and could barely function, so such assumptions only aggravated the already dire circumstance. Over time, I realised that I owed no one any explanation, nor could I control what people said or thought. I chose to work on my emotions and owned the process as time went on.

We watched the first year go by, then the second. No pregnancy symptoms were in sight.

***

Back in 1998, when I was posted to Port Harcourt for my National Youth Service Corps (NYSC), a programme designed for youths to serve the country after tertiary education and before seeking proper paid jobs, my desire was to work in the oil and gas industry. As an undergraduate I had a clear goal, which was to make sure I served the nation in a city where I could get a permanent job afterwards. This did not work out when and how I thought it would. Most of those who started off NYSC with me got teaching or banking opportunities, while I turned down all offers and waited for my dream job in the oil and gas industry. Soon after, I got a job with an oil servicing company, which I was excited about, but I dropped it as fast as I got it. I realised it was a one-man business that was not as structured as I had desired, and the last thing I wanted was to start off on a wrong note. I had to change my strategy and looked for alternatives.

Unenthusiastically I started working with a merchant bank when nothing better came up in the oil and gas sector. I turned down all offers I got from commercial banks at that time because I wanted a balanced life and did not plan to spend endless hours at work. I believed the merchant banks dealt with big-ticket transactions and would require less time at work. Before the service year ended, I had interviewed for about five different jobs. It appeared many of us were interested in making a living from the oil and gas sector, so the chances of getting a job with one were slim. After a little over a year in the merchant bank, I realised the work hours were practically the same, with less income compared to the commercial banks. That sounded an alarm within me as I started a job search. One of the offers I got was in a commercial bank, which I did not hesitate to take up while praying and keeping hope alive for the oil and gas sector.

Late one afternoon almost two years into our marriage, I found I had no cheques or deposit slips to post. It was rare for business to be so light that operations staff like me had an opportunity to leave the bank during the workday. In addition, the bank's internet systems were down, which was usual. This afforded me an opportunity to cross over to the bank across the road from mine where a close friend worked, just to say hello. My friend Chinwe and I met during NYSC and both served in the same merchant bank. She studied chemical engineering in the university and also wanted to work in the oil and gas industry. We had similar aspirations and had grown into bosom friends in the process. She got married right after NYSC, and I happened to be her chief bridesmaid. Like me, she had settled for a job in a commercial bank, and though we worked less than 300 metres from each other, the demanding nature of our jobs made us strangers.

She was excited to see me and was certain I had come to share some news with her. She teased me that I was finally settled, as a lot of openings in my field had recently been advertised in the dailies by some oil and gas companies.

'What?' I exclaimed. 'Why didn't you reach out to me?'

'You mean you didn't see it?' she responded.

She knew I desired a job in the oil and gas industry; also, I rarely read newspapers daily because I found them boring. I was sad to have missed such an opportunity. I enquired further and was told the period for submitting applications had closed the week before I paid Chinwe a visit.

Though disappointed, the spirit of positivity was aroused in me, and something in me refused to just give up. I was certain I had nothing to lose by applying anyway.

At this time, online platforms were non-existent, and applications were manually submitted. The next day, I picked up my pen, wrote an application, attached my Curriculum Vitae and was ready to have it dispatched to the company that had advertised. After all, I only had paper, ink and dispatch fees to lose in that mission. I had hoped the bank's dispatch rider could assist in dropping off the application, but he was too busy. I was not ready to let another day slip by, so I appealed to one of the bank's cleaning personnel, Emmanuel, to assist me. When he arrived at the company, he made enquiries at the gate and in the process realised the application period had been extended by a week; ergo, my application was submitted. It was only a first step, yet my joy knew no bounds. I was ecstatic.

The suspense began. Would I be shortlisted? Did I qualify? I remember the advertisements stated an added advantage was being a member of an accounting professional body. I was not registered or a member of any such body at the time. I realised that some friends and acquaintances, most of whom were qualified professional accountants, had also applied to the same company for the same or similar roles. Just the thought of it made me feel unqualified, but I shoved it aside and kept my eyes on the finish line. There was no giving up or looking back. I had my faith button activated, as I was certain the race was not by my power or might. I needed to trust God completely.

I continued to take my banking role seriously, guarding the bird-in-hand jealously while staying positive about the one in the bush. I didn't have to wait too long. A couple of weeks later, I got an invitation notifying me that I had been shortlisted for the interview process. I was overjoyed and danced as if I'd just won a lottery. It was another step in the right direction. I'd started reading journals that suited the job position I applied for even before I was shortlisted, and only continued with the process. I remained positive throughout the recruitment exercise. I wasn't too sure how it would go, but I was assured that whatever the case might be, God had my back!

The recruitment process had three stages. The first was a written test which was held in the company's cafeteria. There were so many candidates that it was scary. I gave it my best shot and was at peace. Thankfully, I made it and was shortlisted. The second phase interviews had three sessions: with the HR team, a psychologist, and the technical team. I went back to the drawing board and studied harder than I did for my finals in the university. Soon afterwards, the results came out. I made it!

Only one more hurdle to cross. Many people, who were more qualified, in my opinion, did not scale through and had dropped out of the race. The last interview was scheduled for a day after my birthday. I usually looked forward to my birthday each year. It's a day I would always reflect, be thankful, cook, and plan something fun. For those who loved my cooking, it was an open house, and anyone was free to drop by and share my day with me. 13 July 2003 was different. I spent the day fasting and praying.

I had a strong urge to dedicate my birthday to God in preparation for what was ahead. It was just about doing something different for a different kind of result. My final interview was scheduled for the next day, 14 July, 2003, and I arrived in my brown skirt suit with my hair all nicely packed up, feeling confident enough for the task ahead. I was given two topics and allotted a time slot to prepare and present to the senior management of the company. One of the topics was a relatively practical topic I could easily talk about, but the second one was on investment decision methods, which I had never enjoyed. I went in boldly to see the panellist when the time was right. I answered all the questions as best as I could, and when I was asked to present the two topics, I knew I was in for some fumbling. I spoke so well about the topic I was familiar with and chose to stay quiet on the other, hoping it would be overlooked; that did not happen. I struggled through, smiling, and concluded that the toughest of all stages was the final stage. I left there praying, thanking God for the opportunity and hoping for the best. I was anxious.

Unlike the feedback from all other stages that came within weeks, this time there was a long silence. My husband and I had our first vacation as a couple planned for August 2003, and I had hoped I would get some feedback before the trip, but it was not forthcoming. Looking forward to the trip kept me distracted, but it was difficult to erase my expectations.

Just before the trip, I learned through a friend that one of the interviewees had been offered a job. I still had not heard from the company and was not certain of the number of openings available. My heart sank! As I encouraged myself in the Lord, so did my husband encourage me. He asked that I learn from his journey thus far, and yes indeed, there was a lot to learn. I braced up and continued to live.

Surprisingly, seven months later, I got an offer from the company. By that time, I had totally given up. I had no clue I was kept in view as the second-best candidate and was offered a place when another role opened. My joy knew no bounds. I just could not help appreciating God for His faithfulness. Finally, my job mission to Port Harcourt was achieved. I was quick to share this testimony in the church where I worshipped.

17 years later, I still work for this company

***

Back to waiting for a baby, right? Three years passed, then four. It appeared there was no movement or traction. It was time to go back to history and do a review and possibly begin to seek medical help. I recalled an incident that occurred back in 1999, while I was working at the merchant bank. I had felt something wet dripping down my legs. I was a bit startled as I was not expecting my monthly period. A quick check showed it was a grey-coloured fluid, which even scarier. I rushed off to the bathroom and still could not figure out what was going on. Fearful, I left for the hospital immediately. The doctor referred me to an imaging centre. Other than chest X-rays, I had never had any other scan done, so it was all strange to me. The radiographer asked that I drink a lot of water because he could only get good results once my bladder was full. The scan showed I had an enlarged womb. The next few questions were a bit baffling:

Radiographer: 'Did you just undergo an abortion?'

Me: 'No.'

Radiographer: 'Have you ever been pregnant?'

Me: 'No.'

Radiographer: 'Why are you young girls always lying?'

Me: 'What? Are you all right? Are you my dad or my mum? What do I have to gain or lose by lying to you? Will you focus on your duties and stop being ridiculous?'

I was visibly upset. I doubt I had ever felt that insulted. I was kind enough to ask him if he was done with the assessment, sprang up from the bed and was ready for the results.

After all the drama, the report showed I had a growth that looked like a cyst on my cervix. I was referred to a gynaecologist, who asked that I return to the clinic in two days for a surgery. I was scared, as the only sickness I knew was dysmenorrhoea. I am not sure how, but I contacted my mum, who immediately requested that I get all the results and proceed to Calabar, where she had an experienced gynaecologist and I could be properly cared for.

I took time off work and went off to Calabar. The surgery was done under partial anaesthesia. The doctor described what I had as a cervical polyp. It was a benign growth with the tendency of recurring. It was an outpatient surgery, and I was able to go home as soon as the anaesthesia wore off. The doctor recommended that I get myself a mature, and preferably much older, boyfriend really quick. The choice of a much older boyfriend was inspired by all the talking I did during the surgery. He found me quite assertive and thought that a man my age might find it difficult to put me in check. How funny! He also recommended that should I get pregnant while at it, I should make sure to keep it as I would likely have fertility issues.

I remember leaving that hospital with a resolve never to return to that doctor, not even for follow-up checks. His ideologies did not align with my beliefs and values. In retrospect, I wondered if that condition could have been the reason for my inability to get pregnant. On the other hand, my husband had gone through two surgeries at different times for varicoceles. Varicoceles are linked to poor-functioning valves in veins around the testicular area and can lead to terrible pain. It was difficult to know where the problem was, as we both had peculiar circumstances that could contribute to infertility.

While we processed the various challenges and attempted to resolve them, the waiting continued. For a lot of ladies and, in some cases, couples, that is the most gruelling time. There is this all-eyes-on-me feeling that is difficult to explain. In challenging times, it is interesting how a lot of negativity and unimpressive stories surround you. There would be unsolicited advisers—some good, some bad but supposedly with a common goal. You need to be intentional about listening to only positive news by choosing your friends and acquaintances wisely, meditating on God's Word and constantly renewing your mind.

An elderly colleague made a cynical comment roughly three years after Tobin and I married: 'Rather than go settle down and have a baby, you are smiling all over the place and shaking your tiny waist.' Surprisingly, I didn't take any offence or feel bad. It showed that I was not wearing my problems on my face or as an outfit. That made me feel good. I shared that experience with my boss at the time, who eventually became a close friend. She was upset and wondered why anyone should talk that carelessly. I could understand her concern. She had waited seven years to have her first child, so she could relate to what I was dealing with. I found time to give the elderly colleague feedback and cautioned her about speaking carelessly, especially when she had no history of the person in question.

The Bible admonishes us to cast our burdens on the Lord. Most times we say we have handed it over, but we rarely act like we have. The encounter with the lady made me believe I acted it out well, such that all she saw was a joyful heart.

Several advisers showed up with all manner of suggestions: Your tummy is too hot. You need a massage to position your womb. There is a woman who will pray for you over a three-day period, but you need to wear a sackcloth. The list was endless. I appreciated the various advisers; they meant well and were truly concerned, but I found some of their recommended routes rather weird because they were not biblical and lacked the scientific backing to prove them right or wrong, as the case may be. I had to keep reminding myself that indeed, 'My people perish for lack of knowledge', as the Bible says. I just couldn't reconcile going to a village, sleeping on the floor, not brushing my teeth for three days, or wearing a sackcloth as the solution for having a baby. Where have works ever translated to grace?

While waiting, I decided this could be an interesting or frustrating time, depending on how I chose to approach it. I tried not to get upset. I made it a point of duty to thank people for their concern and assured them there was nothing to worry about. I always reminded them that my husband and I had decided to trust in God. If I found anyone overbearing, I chose to avoid them to forestall any unpleasant confrontation. After all is said and done, the ball falls right back in one's court. Who are you? What promises are you holding on to? What do you value? What do you believe? It is always best to know who you are in Christ and what His promises are.

***

My husband and I had yet another vacation to the US planned for October 2005. At this time, we had decided to establish what could be medically wrong in order to understand exactly what we were dealing with. We mentioned this to my sister-in-law Onsu, my husband's immediate younger sister and a lawyer who lived in Washington, DC. She promised to do some research on doctors and possibly schedule an appointment for us, since we planned to stop by at her home for a few days. As an efficient lady, she saw it through.

On 25 October 2005, we had an appointment with a highly recommended doctor in Washington, DC. It was a cold day and a long, interesting walk to the doctor's office. We hoped we would be able to find our way there safely, as we had never walked the streets of Washington, DC, prior to this visit. At first, we strictly followed the directions we had printed from MapQuest, the predecessor to Google Maps, but soon we discovered how easy it was to move around due to the grid system of the streets.

The doctor, a urologist who specialised in fertility issues, was ready and waiting to see his clients from Africa. With just a few questions, review of our medical records, brief physical exam and results of a test carried out in his clinic, the next definite proclamation by him was, 'It is impossible for you two to have a child naturally'. Before we could catch our breath, he went on to say that in vitro fertilisation (IVF) was not an option and would be unsuccessful. The only likely option proposed was an intracytoplasmic sperm injection (ICSI). That was new terminology to us, so he explained that it involves injecting an individual sperm cell into an egg cell. He went on to advise that we go explore that option in Europe, as it would be an extremely expensive venture in the US.

As unpleasant as the news from the doctor was, all I remember saying as we came down the stairs of the medical building was God's Word that said, 'There shall be none barren in my land, neither male nor female'. I quoted that to my husband and felt at ease, because at that point it was clear that it didn't matter which of us had a problem. All that mattered was that God's got our backs! We left the clinic acting like we just got the best news ever. We stopped by a Chinese fast-food restaurant, got ourselves a meal and took yet another interesting walk back to our accommodation.

Three days after we returned to Nigeria, our pastor and his lovely wife had an awesome gift that was being dedicated to God in a church service. This was a baby who was birthed after ten years of waiting. This special couple had been told natural conception was not possible, but then God did it. I remember just getting to the parking lot in church, dressed in a lilac-coloured lace fabric made into a long skirt and blouse, when my phone rang; it was my boss-turned-friend, Amara. She said good-humoredly, 'I hope you are properly dressed'. When I wondered why, she went on to say that Mrs. Ugoh, the miracle baby's mother, wished for me to dance out with her daughter, Demilade. I laughed out loud and assured her I was sleek enough for the special assignment. When it got to the dedication segment of the service, I was privileged to be asked to carry the miracle baby to the altar for prayers. I was excited, danced and carried the baby with expectation, keying into that special miracle.

***

As we had been advised to try alternative methods of conception, I put calls through to a fertility hospital in Nigeria and made inquiries on how much the basic IVF procedure would cost, the duration of the procedure, as well as to ask all the other necessary questions. This was not because I had plans of having the procedure carried out at the time, but I needed to channel my prayers properly. I remember I was given a bill of approximately 500,000 Naira, roughly $5,000 at the time. Good information for the next steps.

The story of Hannah in the Bible and how she prayed for a child was a frequent reference point for me. She had promised to have the child serve God if He would answer her prayer. I remember making a vow during a midweek service. My vow was not complicated and was specific. I placed a demand on the Almighty Father, asking that He bless us with a child so I could bring the sum quoted for the IVF to the church for the furtherance of the Gospel. For the record, there is absolutely nothing wrong with IVF if a couple decides to go that route. I see IVF as God's intervention, as He gave the doctors the wisdom to come up with it in the first place.

Tobin and I just dreamt of a different path.

CHAPTER THREE

Oh Wow!

We had just been ushered into a new year, 2006, and it was that time of the year for setting targets, making resolutions and earnestly working towards realising them. We had just celebrated our fourth wedding anniversary too, and it was only normal to reflect on life as a couple and set short- and medium-term goals together. One action point from our discussions was to go for the long overdue follow-up appointment that had been fixed by the urologist who performed a surgery on my husband in 2005. At some point, we had thought it wasn't necessary to go back for the check-up; however, considering the unpromising report we had received from the doctor in the US, we thought it wise, at least, to offer him a response.

With the euphoria of following up on action points from a new year's plan, we set out in the first week of January to the urologist's office, though somewhere deep down I wished we started off with something more exciting and less sensitive. It was mid-morning on a Saturday when we got to the clinic. The doctor was soft-spoken, and there always seemed to be an aura of peace around him. He was all ears and listened calmly as we recounted the visit to the doctor in the US and his recommended solution. He simply told us that only one sperm was needed to get an egg fertilised, not millions. He advised that we stay positive, irrespective of the news or report we had received. Just before we rounded up the conversation, he asked me when last I had my monthly period. That was when it dawned on me that my period was slightly delayed and should have come sometime between the third and fourth week of December. I told him I wasn't sure and even cracked a joke that, who knows, I might be pregnant, and we all chuckled. The consultation ended with no medications or further recommendations. We stepped out without answers but with an assurance that everything would be fine.

The days went by, then a week or two more, and it became obvious that my monthly cycle was nowhere in sight. Excitement welled up within me because I had never missed a period, so this had to be good news. It just had to be! I needed to run a test, but the thought of just going to the clinic to ask for a pregnancy test felt absurd. I mused over leisurely walking to a clinic I had never used to have a test done just to help manage my expectations. I did not feel different, wasn't sick, and didn't want to draw unnecessary attention to myself. Walking into a pharmacy and requesting a home test kit seemed like a more comfortable option, and that was what I did. I bought the test strips on our way home from work one evening and anxiously waited for the next morning as was recommended at the time for higher reliability. It felt like the night lasted forever; each time I woke up to check the time, the hands of the clock had barely moved. I doubt the cock crowed before I was in the bathroom to do the test, and my husband was just a few steps behind. We patiently waited till we saw the two pink ticks that confirmed I was pregnant.

Oh wow! What a relief!

I was ecstatic, full of joy, confused, thankful, thrilled, shocked and almost doubtful. The emotions were not much different for my husband, just a calmer more composed version. All we could say was, 'Thank you, Lord'. We both wondered if it was a dream. We stepped out that day with that feeling that overtakes you when you know what no one else does. It was our little big secret!

Roughly two weeks later, I felt bolder. I went to the industrial clinic at my office and requested for a confirmatory pregnancy test. It came out positive yet again.

I remained dazed, as it was difficult to comprehend that less than three months after a doctor of great renown and expertise had declared natural conception impossible, with no intervention, not even folic acid, I was confirmed pregnant. All praise and glory to Him who reigns.

It was a whole new world to me, and I looked forward to every step of the pregnancy journey. As the weeks went by, I expected some nausea. It never happened. I expected to get tired. Neither did that happen. I only noticed that I expanded sideways, my skin glowed nicely, and I just enjoyed the entire process. If I had not done two pregnancy tests, I probably would have still doubted I was pregnant, as all the expectations from stories told and untold did not happen. I just felt good.

Things seemed to be falling into place. We had moved into a self-owned property the previous year. Coincidentally, we'd bought a grade A, fairly used car towards the end of the previous year, and it was on its way from the United States. The timing was perfect for the expected baby, as the overused gold Toyota Carina II we had owned for a little over three years had seen better days. The car, which we called 'Edo Line' (nicknamed after the Edo State road transport company, with its fleet of overworked cars), was bought in Edo State when my husband worked in Benin briefly. It had served its purpose but had started falling apart.

We practised the power of silence with this pregnancy. Other than our pastor and very few family members, we decided not to let anyone know till after the twelfth week. Tobin and I used that season to keep exercising the faith we shared as a couple, speaking and declaring what we believed as often as we could. We left everyone to the guessing game. While we kept praying, trusting and speaking, I read a lot of impactful books: *Supernatural Childbirth*, *What to Expect When You Are Expecting* and many more.

My employer was a joint venture with an operation base in Port Harcourt, but with partners in Lagos. Periodically, budgets and performance had to be defended with partners prior to approvals or authorisation to spend. Before the twelfth week of the pregnancy, I had to go on an official trip to Lagos for three days to defend a few dossiers with the company's partners. The trip went well and most approvals given, and I was scheduled to return to Port Harcourt the next day.

Just when I was heading to my room via a slightly raised slope, I missed a step, tripped and fell—or more like performed an involuntary split. I sobbed, though I was uncertain if it was borne out of pain or pity. I panicked and hoped my little big secret was still intact. All appeared okay till I woke up the next day to get ready for the airport and realised I was bleeding lightly or spotting, as they usually refer to it. Some form of fear stepped in and the anxiety started. Had the worst happened? Does this spell danger?

I struggled to stay focused as I travelled back to Port Harcourt but kept praying under my breath. When I arrived at my destination, though a weekend, I headed to the industrial clinic at my office while putting a call through to the midwife, as I reckoned the service would be skeletal. I was immediately referred to a retainer hospital that had a lot of gynaecologists. I scampered off to the clinic, not wanting to take any chances. The nurse had called the hospital prior to my arrival to ensure they attended to me urgently. As soon as I arrived, the speed with which the registration process happened was impressive. The gynaecologist examined me and carried out an ultrasound immediately. She assured me there was nothing to worry about but admitted me all the same to ensure I rested and got followed up properly. I was discharged from the hospital two days later, and thankfully that was the end of the drama. The pregnancy was confirmed as being intact.

Was it really the end of the drama? Maybe with the pregnancy, but it didn't seem life would stand still and watch me cruise.

***

Our new car, a blue Honda CRV, arrived in February 2006. A nice car it was, and when compared to our very own Edo Line, it was heavenly. It thrilled us! On the 18th of March, barely a month later, Tobin and I were on our way for a friend's daughter's first birthday. The traffic light at the popular Water Lines junction in Port Harcourt had gone red, and while we waited patiently for the light to turn green, we heard a loud bang from our rear. A Mercedes Benz, then referred to as the Baby Benz, had run into us. The immediate reaction was shock, then some form of anger but luckily not rage. It jolted us no doubt, but we were stable enough to step out for an assessment. Thankfully, the damage to our car was minor compared to the car that ran into us. We had to send the car to the garage for repairs immediately, as we had a trip planned for 14 April. The rejected Edo Line became our fallback option.

The car made it back in good time for our trip, and shortly after we returned, we needed to attend the service of songs for a friend's mum, which was scheduled for 21 April, 2006. I hitched a ride home from work with a colleague, stopped briefly at the venue of the service of songs, and walked home thereafter. The place was very close to where we lived, so my husband and I planned to take a walk back there when he returned from work. I expected him back before it got dark. When he had not shown up at 6.30pm and there was power failure, I put on the generator and tried to get other home chores sorted.

Less than an hour later, I heard a creaking sound which was an indicator that the gate to our house was being opened. Usually I would have rushed off to open the door and welcome my husband, as he was the only one who could drive in, or so I thought, but something kept me in check this time, and without knowing why or what it was, I waited for a knock first. The knock did not come through as fast as I expected it to. Then I heard some voices, or more like a conversation, right by my bedroom window. My heart skipped! *Who could that be?* I wondered, because we lived alone. *Oh, possibly the security guard?* My curiosity got the better of me, so I peeped through the window. Out there was a young man with what looked like a gun pointed at someone on the ground, who looked like my husband. Then I looked further and saw another man holding the security guard captive. At that point, I knew we were in for an adventure.

Fear gripped me, but I knew I needed to act fast. I turned off the light in the room where I peeped from, so I could see the invaders, while they couldn't see me. I got my phone, crept under the bed and started frantically dialling phone numbers for security agencies for help. None of them picked up as fast as I desired. I was shaken when I could not get through to the help lines, but

I reached a few people who could help contact them.

Between calls, I sneaked right back to the window to monitor what was going on. I heard the young man with the gun ask who was in the house. I heard my husband say there was no one at home. There I was with the power generating set making a lot of noise, wondering who would believe such a story when spirits don't turn on generators.

We lived in an area called Mgbuoba/NTA Road. It was quite notorious for criminal activities, and car snatching had become the order of the day. We had no personal negative encounter or stories before this fateful day when the security guard was overpowered as he tried to grant access to his employer. We heard stories that had stayed as stories. There it was, happening right before my eyes and scaring the living daylights out of me.

I finally got through to a security agency, and the next task was giving directions to and a description of the property. It was a tough task describing the route to take, landmarks etc. Port Harcourt is not the best in town planning, and GPS was not functional in Nigeria at the time. After what seemed like forever, I heard the sound of a car leaving the premises. I peeped again and saw our barely-two-months-owned vehicle being driven out. I was not sure who was at the wheel, but my husband no longer lay on the ground. I panicked yet again and hoped they had not pulled out with him in the car. Still afraid of stepping out, I continued calling for help. Apparently, the robbers locked him up in the restroom at the security house before making away with the car. I only realised this when Tobin forced himself out of the place and started running after the car.

What an awful experience that was! The security agents showed up about 20 minutes after the car had been stolen. All attempts to recover the vehicle failed. Thankfully, the car had a comprehensive insurance cover, which helped ease the financial burden.

Osunyameye: Nothing is Impossible with God

It was a hard pill to swallow. Life continued while we went back to our Edo Line.

***

Insomnia was a word I had heard ever so often, but I'd wondered how people worried to the point of sleeplessness. Well, that was the new me. Joyfully pregnant yet afraid of men from the underworld! Fear had taken over my entire being. I spent nights listening out for noises. I could no longer return home alone at night. If my husband was caught up at work, I would wait at a colleague's house till he was done and could come get me. I tried all I could to fight the fear, prayed all I could, read all I could. Those helped a lot, but I guess the pregnancy hormones were working overtime, and a sense of peace at that time remained elusive.

In between the fears, we sought normalcy, tried to live life as usual, but we were only successful during the daytime, when I could see and decipher all sounds around and within me.

Thankfully, I was kept busy with preparations for the baby, which mildly put, is a full-time job for a first-time expectant mother. We had planned to travel out of the country for the birth. The primary reason was for good medical care but then again for the attendant benefits for the child in creating future opportunities. I had heard stories of people being turned back from the United States because they were obviously pregnant; some airports were notorious for doing that, even when you had cogent reasons and could demonstrate you could foot your bills. Because of this, just figuring out the 'costume' to travel out with and the hairdo for the long-haul flight was enough to keep me busy. I just wanted to be admitted into the United States effortlessly without my integrity being compromised.

I made several enquiries and contacted my sister-in-law Onsu, who by this time had moved from Washington, DC, to Maryland. She assured me that our plan was not illegal, advised that I pay my bills and ensure I kept my receipts properly.

We even agreed that I would fly in through DC, so she could be close by if anything went unexpectedly wrong.

In the first week of August 2006, I left for the United States. I hadn't tried to disguise myself other than wearing red lipstick and purple eyeshadow. I remember wearing my husband's chequered shirt for this trip, as it seemed to be the only comfortable outfit around. When we landed at Dulles International, the lady right next to me at the immigration counter was being challenged on why she was coming into the US with a 32-week pregnancy, which I found surprising. I even wondered how they possibly knew, as she did not look pregnant at all and was wearing a fitted dress. There I was at 35 weeks pregnant, my tummy really protruding but my face unaltered, and no one interrogated me. My passport was stamped, and I just went through. It could only have been God's divine favour.

Everything went smoothly, right from my first night. Onsu was at the airport to get me to her lovely home in the nice neighbourhood of Silver Spring, where I planned to spend a few days before proceeding to Atlanta to be with my eldest brother and his family. I slept so well, like I had never done three months prior. The change of environment seemed to have played a huge role that ended the cycle of fear and sleeplessness. It was a new birth, a new me.

CHAPTER FOUR

Time to Expect the Expected

I arrived in Atlanta three days later and settled in with my brother Tambu and his family. I had done a lot of research to find a good doctor while back home in Nigeria. As a cash-paying patient without medical insurance, I needed a facility that would take it into consideration, give a decent bill and stay professional.

A dependable family friend whom I fondly call 'Chichi of KC Healthcare', a nickname coined from a voicemail, referred me to a doctor. Coincidentally, her sister, who lived in the United Kingdom, had just been delivered of a baby by the doctor she recommended in the United States. His practice impressed her with their high quality service. I had contacted his office while in Nigeria, and he was willing to take over the prenatal care at 35 weeks, to the extent that I had no complications and could send in my medical notes. That suited me perfectly, and I had scheduled an appointment prior to my arrival in the United States.

A major concern was how to move around. I had not driven in the US before, and other than downtown Atlanta, where public transportation was effective, the suburbs had only taxis that were expensive. Courtesy of Ada, my brother's wife, yet another helpful sister-in-law, moving around was taken care of. She gladly drove me to the doctor's office for my first and subsequent appointments.

She had to bring along my three-year-old nephew, Ata. The appointment went better than I expected. I was attended by a welcoming receptionist and a cheerful professional doctor of Ghanaian descent. There was no cause for alarm, as everything looked perfectly okay from the ultrasound scans that were taken. The ''expected' was bubbly and fine!

According to other mothers I knew, the time to do all the shopping was while the baby was nicely tucked away in my womb. I had been strongly advised to make sure I tidied up all I needed to, because it would not be so easy once the baby arrived. Ada was wonderful. She had attained this feat well in advance and was experienced enough to guide me. We moved from shop to shop, loving the pink outfits that always created a bed of roses in my mind's eye but sticking to the unisex outfits, as we had chosen not to learn the sex of our baby prior to birth. My husband and mum arrived in the following weeks, and the shopping party grew. By day we shopped, and in the evenings we sorted our purchases.

Our baby's expected date of delivery was 15 September 2006, so I had weekly checks from when I arrived, and each time I had a doctor's visit, he performed scans. I had an appointment on 12 September, to which my husband, mum and Ada accompanied me. When a physical exam was done, my cervix seemed to have dilated slightly. The doctor explained a new concept to me, which he referred to as a finger sweep. It involved running a finger around the cervix to trigger contractions, which would eventually lead to the birthing of the baby. Apparently, it is performed in the very early stage of dilation. He performed the finger sweep and recommended I have my packed hospital bags handy, which I already did, as the experts—my mum and Ada—had prompted. I would be required to find my way back to the clinic whenever I started experiencing frequent contractions or serious labour pains, as the sweep was most likely to kick-start labour sooner than expected.

As he predicted, I had barely left his office when I started feeling cramps in the lower part of my tummy. *Could that be contractions?* My experts confirmed it most likely was. It started as bearable discomfort and progressively altered my pain threshold. At that point, what better way to be distracted than strolling in a mall? I loved combing shops for good deals as a way of whiling away time. We went off to Discover Mills, now known as Sugarloaf Mills, the largest outlet mall in Georgia. Nothing prepared me for the intense pain that followed shortly after. Ada asked that I keep walking around till it was unbearable so I wouldn't have to wait too long in the hospital before the baby came. Great advice, but tough to implement.

With the intense pain I was already dealing with, I kept walking around in an uncoordinated manner. We made a stop at Off Broadway Shoe Warehouse, and just when we started making our way out of the shop, I felt hot fluid gush out from between my thighs, right down to my feet. I got confused for a second then suddenly realised that my water had just broken, a term I had only heard and read about. I was transfixed! My mum and Tobin rushed to the restroom to get some tissue paper for a quick clean, while I stood with my legs tightly joined, like I was safeguarding the baby from falling out. It was an unmistakable sign that we needed to return to the hospital instantly.

Did I mention intense pain earlier? It was nothing in comparison to what I felt by the time I reached the labour room. I remember my husband encouraging me to bear the pain, reminding me of how I'd always dealt with serious, painful dysmenorrhoea over the years. *How are they even related?* I wondered. Dysmenorrhoea was child's play by comparison. How do women go through such excruciating pain over and over — even nine, ten, eleven times?

I guess it has to do with the joy that welled up within me when I was delivered of a lovely baby girl on 12 September, 2006 at 6.18pm. A simply amazing feeling that I will always struggle to find words to explain. A feeling that vastly occupied where the birth pains had been and beyond. All praise and glory to the Most High God!

We spent a night in the hospital, the equivalent of a five-star hotel, to satisfy the mandatory 24-hour period needed to monitor the baby and take some blood samples to run various tests. The next evening, Tambu picked us up and drove us back to his house.

Such a joy, such a relief. As a first-timer I was excited to have my mum around; I needed any help offered. I wasn't shy to ask, and I was very grateful for any rendered. I was bent on breastfeeding exclusively for six months. I struggled initially but pushed right through, and I was glad I did.

On the eighth day, our dear Pastor Chris Ugoh performed the Christian naming rights over the phone and prayed for her. We named her Innomama Osunyameye Fabiawari Dickson, each name deliberately chosen to reflect the journey and our victory. There is a meaning behind all of them:

Innomama: Her dad named her after his late mum. It literally means 'Don't cheat me' in Kalabari, but we chose to have it interpreted as 'I like justice'.

Osunyameye: That was my name for her, a Ghanaian name. Her late paternal grandad was Ghanaian. I struggled to find a name reflective of our journey so far as a couple and could not agree more with this one, which I stole from her aunt Onsu. It simply means, 'Nothing is impossible with God'. I was very intentional about this name, as the doctor had clearly told us it was impossible to have a child naturally.

Fabiawari: That was the name her special great-aunt Gubsie, who has continued to play the role of her paternal grandmother, gave her. It means, 'the one on which the house is built'.

The days went by, and adjusting to life with a new baby had its own challenges. Innomama loved eating but probably loved crying more. I recall my dear friend Eruvy visiting and spending a sleepless night because the baby just would not stop crying. She cooed and sang to the baby, quickly making up lovely songs to manage the crying and help pacify the baby, but to no avail.

Other than a scary phone call from the hospital stating she had sickle cell trait—which I misinterpreted as sickle cell disease—everything else was fine, and we had clearance to return to Nigeria.

CHAPTER FIVE

The Next 21 Months

We had our plans firmed up to return to Nigeria as a party of four, but that got thwarted when we got to the airport and realised the newbie mum did not have all the papers for baby Innomama. My husband and mum had to go ahead of us, while we stayed back to have her travel documents sorted out. In the confusion I forgot to remove from my husband's bag the 20 bottles of the popular liquid infant milk Enfamil that I had been permitted to have in my carry-on since I was travelling with a baby. All 20 bottles were thrown away by the security team, further aggravating our already bad situation. I had planned for that milk five months down the line when the exclusive breastfeeding journey would be over, but alas, my plans were all ruined. Disappointing, but we waded through another week.

All set and ready this time, we made it to the airport and, with no glitches, flew right into Lagos with plans of returning to Port Harcourt the next day. We got off the plane and waited for what seemed like forever to get our suitcases, which we soon came to realise hadn't made it to Nigeria. I had to spend an extra day with a family friend in Lagos, as I had to return to the airport the following day to pick up my luggage. The night went by rather slowly, and the next day was even slower. I returned to the airport later in the day, and thankfully my luggage was located.

We returned to Port Harcourt after the second night in Lagos, wishing to meet hot, steaming pepper soup, but alas, it didn't quite happen. My mum, done with international 'omugwo', a term used to describe a grandmother or relative taking up the nanny role for a newborn, had returned to her base in Calabar. It felt good to be home in my corner and baby Innomama's unused space outside the belly.

Innomama settled quickly into the new environment. Her lovely bassinet, courtesy of Aunty Maryann, an old friend of mine, was all set up. Maryann and I attended the same secondary school, Federal Government Girls College, Benin City. We shared rides to and from school many times. Through us, our families became friends. She even started off with me in the University of Calabar but won the visa lottery and moved to America after just a year. She got married a year after I did, and we were both expectant mothers. She was determined to get something good for my baby, which she did: a bassinet from Babies 'R' Us, a one-stop shop for baby items.

The sturdy bassinet held Innomama still for brief naps, but I struggle to remember whether she ever slept for more than an hour at a stretch. She would always wake up to eat or cry. I hoped it would stop sooner, but that continued for as long as I can remember. Sleeping through the night was impossible. Caring for a newborn was an enormous task.

Deciding on an elderly or young nanny was yet another task. I was spared that hassle for six months, as my youngest sister, Okaja, fondly known as 'Ok-jaz', got an internship in Port Harcourt, which turned out to be to my advantage. She took care of Innomama as her own daughter. She mastered the act of thawing and feeding her expressed breast milk and much more. Whenever Ok-jaz was home, I could steal some naps and avert the headaches from the sleepless nights. Eventually, when I returned to work after my maternity leave, I could focus at work and be at peace. The nanny business came up much later, but it was an easier slide.

Innomama developed rather quickly, grew round and chubby, which earned her a nickname from her dad: 'Dum Dum', now Dumi. She always wore a big, charming smile when not fussing over anything, which endeared her to many people. She started walking when she was eight months old. She took it a step further by talking. Now, it was not just baby talk; she said things one could understand. If you asked her a simple question at that age like, 'How are you?', you immediately got a response: 'I am pine'. It always sounded so funny because we believed that was rather too early to talk. I wondered then if she understood what she said, or could she just have been repeating what she heard people say? No one knows.

Though a cheerful child, Innomama was quite clingy. We probably contributed to her clingy nature because after waiting and having a child almost in our fifth year of marriage, it was normal to give her all the attention and as many privileges as possible. We promptly attended to her cries, we rocked her to sleep, and she found it easy to sleep on Mum and Dad's bed. After all, she was a queen in her own right.

Just before she turned ten months old, they opened a crèche for female employees' children within my office premises. The crèche had a maximum capacity of ten children and catered for -ages zero to 12 months. This was a welcome idea, especially for mothers with three-month-old babies or younger who had just returned from maternity leave and were still nursing. It would be easy to dash off during lunchtime to check on the baby. It was a bit late in the day for us, though. My sister Ok-jaz had long returned to school, and after a fair share of trials and failures in getting a trusted helping hand, we had now settled for a reliable nanny called Glory, whose presence ushered in some stability to our schedule. Innomama and Glory had taken to each other so well that we were apprehensive about embracing the new opportunity.

We braced up all the same and thought it wise to have Innomama mix with other children early enough to make pre-kindergarten easier to manage. We thought it through, applied for a spot at the crèche and got it approved. She became my new companion to work every other day. We settled for a blended format where she only had to be at the crèche on alternate days. Her first day was disappointing. She cried so much that I wondered if the decision to get her enrolled was a good one.

We survived the first week and hoped things would ease off, but Innomama continued to cry each time I dropped her off. In fact, she cried each time until she graduated, but we needed it for her development. When she turned one, we had a shindig at the crèche as a way of saying thank you and goodbye. But the office crèche was a novel initiative, and the pioneer babies were few. Since it would take a while to get to the maximum capacity of ten babies, they allowed Innomama to stay on till she got to 15 months. After her stay at the crèche, she was happy to be back home, where she spent three uninterrupted months with the family before she returned to a daycare.

In March 2008, we went on a brief vacation to America. It was a reunion for Innomama and her cousin Ata in Atlanta. They bonded so well and had a good time playing in the park and at home. During that trip, Innomama spiked her first fever. It was rather strange, as not even vaccinations gave her a fever. We had no clue what caused it and were rather confused. It was a reminder that we were first-timers in the baby business, though she was 18 months old.

Ada advised we start off with paracetamol and determine afterwards if we needed to go to the hospital or not. We bought Tylenol over the counter. I remember being rather worried, as we could not quite place our hands on the root cause. She was not teething; her nose wasn't running; her tonsils were not inflamed, so what? We worried more because we had a trip within three days to Washington, DC, and would prefer to make the journey with a healthy child. Thankfully, she responded to Tylenol, and her temperature dropped within acceptable limits.

We continued to Washington, DC, to visit her aunties Onsu and Singto, her dad's younger sisters, who both could not wait to spend time with their niece. Onsu had never met Innomama; the last time we saw each other was when I was pregnant and travelled through Dulles. Singto had visited us in Atlanta when Innomama was born and even had a blog, *Notes from the Hyena's Belly*, where she put up the story of her visit. That was the first time baby Innomama featured on the internet.

We arrived at DC, eager to see Onsu's place as she had moved houses since we last visited. They had a small house party for Tobin, whose birthday was some days earlier. They presented him with a cute chocolate cake with candles on it. Singto had an ear for delightful music and had enough downloads in her device to get a party of five charged up. Innomama was so excited that one could have easily thought it was her birthday. She danced so skillfully in her pink top and white trousers that it got us all cracked up. There was a park close to Onsu's house, which her aunt Singto took her to. She enjoyed playing on the swing. She played with such gusto that we all forgot she had a fever a few days earlier. It was a memorable trip with lots of pictures taken to show for it.

***

We returned to Port Harcourt shortly afterwards and had Innomama enrolled in the daycare arm of Hope Springs School, which was close to where we lived. That was in April 2008. She still got frightened by strangers and continued to cry each time we dropped her off at the daycare. However, she connected well with one of her teachers, Ms. Mary, who knew how best to manage her. She would let no other member of staff pick her up from the gate or reception if Ms. Mary was not available. She wore a different chequered outfit with a cute collar each day, provided by the school. Though the daily reports we got always had the crying or clingy bit, Innomama got home each day with either a new story or some baby work she did in school, which left us with the impression that she enjoyed the activities.

The routine stayed stable until early in May 2008, when she came home walking in a funny way. She wasn't limping, but her legs were bent, and she walked as though she had K-legs. We asked her if she fell, but she said no. We asked if she was in pain; she said no. We followed up with a visit to the school the next day, but it was news to everyone. No one seemed to have observed anything unusual about her. We had no information to work with. With close attention, we noticed she was suddenly silent and withdrawn. She lost appetite too; that was easy to detect because she loved food.

We needed a medical diagnosis. We went on to the clinic, where an X-ray showed nothing significant. They gave her anti-inflammatory medication and some painkillers, and we returned home. We hoped it was over, but apparently it was not. She started running a temperature shortly after. We ran off to the clinic yet again. This time around, some blood tests were run. Her white blood cell count was abnormally high, while malaria and typhoid tests returned negative results. They prescribed some antibiotics for her, and we returned home. She felt better but just wasn't back to Innomama.

Call it a mother's instinct, but I was certain there was more to it. We prayed for clarity and healing. I made sure she completed the recommended dose of the medications she was placed on. There was only a slight improvement, and we watched it for a bit. Coincidentally, the same day she completed the dose of medication, her dad needed to be in Lagos on an official assignment, and we were concluding the purchase of a property that was closer to our offices, as the traffic and crime rate in the axis we lived in was on the rise. Convinced the effect of the drugs would kick in and she would be fine, he travelled as scheduled.

However, the fever returned that night, and Innomama shivered so badly that I thought she was convulsing. She started having loose stools too. I was home with her nanny, Glory, when the symptoms worsened. In my near-helpless state, I called my mum on the phone, who advised I use palm kernel oil on her body. Now, palm kernel oil was quite common, and a lot of mothers with young children had it in their first aid kit. Though with a strong smell, it is believed to have some medicinal value and to be effective in managing convulsion in young children. I had it in my pantry but had never had cause to use it. Glory seemed to be familiar with it and had some quick testimonials to share. I rubbed it on Innomama's body really quickly and rushed off to a paediatric clinic that came highly recommended by a friend. The clinic was not too far from where we lived, so heading there that night seemed like the only viable option. There were quite a few people there, and their turnaround time was commendable, though not without a few glitches. She was admitted immediately, and that was the first time

I had to spend a night in the hospital for a purpose other than having a child.

The hospital ran several blood tests yet again. This time around, the results showed the existence of malaria parasite. Finally, the popular ailment in this part of the world showed up. As was usual practice, the treatments started off right away. I barely closed my eyes before mosquitos started chanting war songs all over the place. I remained confused, as it appeared the hospital was infesting us with malaria rather than treating Innomama. She had medications to be administered intravenously, so opting out was not an option. We survived two more days and then got discharged with medications to continue at home. All that was an exercise in futility, as Innomama was still not herself.

When she still didn't get better after the medications, we returned to the industrial clinic at my office for more analysis. She was admitted immediately, as she had spiked a fever again. Several tests and blood cultures were run. Her red blood cells and haemoglobin levels were low. The white blood cells and ESR (Erythrocyte Sedimentation Rate) were all overboard. Beyond the fever, her eyes appeared swollen. It was getting more complicated, and the maze appeared to be unending, but we were certain there had to be a way out. Finding the way was the task ahead. The clinic became our new home since I commuted to work from there.

Things deteriorated rather quickly. Innomama's blood levels dropped even further, and she needed a transfusion. I had not even had a blood transfusion before, and here I was with a 20-month-old who needed one. How was I supposed to fathom this?

To complicate matters, I had started my accounting professional exams shortly after having Innomama. It was an intensive process, so I took it in little chunks which helped manage my time effectively. I had planned the next set of papers for June 2008, so while caring for a sick child and trying to demystify what was going on,

I was actively preparing for my exams and working on two papers. It was a tough combination, but I was determined to follow through.

Combining everything became increasingly difficult. Tobin and I offered to donate blood to save our baby. They needed to have our blood screened with a sample draw. When it got to my turn, the nurse asked a simple question: 'When last did you have your monthly period?' It was at that point I realised that I had lost track of time; I just couldn't remember. She went on with the blood tests anyway, and of course the tests revealed that I was pregnant with our second child. In a split second I understood that some problems easily overshadow others, because I had no clue whatsoever and had not taken notice of a single pregnancy symptom.

All told, I was not a suitable donor. Thankfully, Tobin's blood tests went well, and he came to the rescue. The blood transfusion went fast enough, with no negative reactions. The next day, new blood tests were run, and her results bounced back with some promise, along with lots of hope. We stayed on in the hospital for further observation. The fever spikes continued, and her appetite remained low, but her energy levels improved.

The medical team wondered why the fever could not be kept under control for more than a few hours. Though the blood cultures yielded no organisms, several cocktails of antibiotics and anaesthetics had been explored. They invited a consultant haematologist who carried out some checks on her blood to understand the behaviour as well as why the levels were dropping so fast.

When the haematologist showed up, I was unavoidably absent. One of my accounting professional papers was scheduled for the same day, and I had gone off to sit for the exams, which started at 9am and ended at noon. Tough paper it was, though some others might have found it straightforward, but I was definitely not in the right state of mind. I was certain I would pass, but maybe not so well. I walked out of the examination hall, hoping the driver who dropped me off earlier in the day would be around to pick me up. The last thing I wanted to do was discuss how I fared at the examinations with other students. I just wanted to leave the scene as fast as I could. However, I was taken aback when I sighted my husband, whom I expected should have been in the hospital with our daughter. In a split second, several questions ran through my head. *Is she all right? Is it getting complicated?* It was impossible to answer any of those questions from afar, because Tobin had a calm demeanour that made it difficult to figure him out.

After the usual 'Hi, sweetie. How were the exams?' kind of pleasantries and questions, he went on to say, 'Nothing is wrong'. The haematologist had done all the checks and said Innomama was fine, but we should get her checked out in another hospital because her blood cells were breaking down so fast or showed an unusual pattern that needed further evaluation. We were referred to a hospital in Lagos for further checks. We needed to hurry because the shuttle bus would leave for the airport in less than three hours. So basically, it had gone beyond Port Harcourt, and it was time to head to Lagos.

We rushed home and got our things packed as quickly as we could. In the process, we were intuitively guided to pick up our international travel documents, as it appeared things were getting more complicated than we could have anticipated—and quickly too. So, it was best to be prepared. We made it right on time to catch the airport shuttle bus from the office. The flight that evening was on schedule, and the medical team had put together a total logistics package, right from Port Harcourt airport to Lagos airport and straight to a renowned hospital which, thankfully, had been notified to expect us. In the meantime, Innomama was busy running all over the place with a wide smile, which gladdened our hearts and made us wonder if the trip was even necessary.

When it was time to see the doctor, we walked right into his office with an active child full of cheer. It was difficult for the doctor to reconcile the dramatic tale of the journey thus far to the little girl he saw in front of him. If not that her case notes had been scanned ahead of our arrival, we probably would have been sent back home, for all the gaiety the little patient was exhibiting. After completing the admission protocol, they assigned Innomama to a room. They ran several tests that night, and we expected results the next day.

We were told the hospital had a UK-trained paediatrician expected to be at work for a proper assessment of the child the next day. We were there for a solution and were open to all available options. The paediatrician showed up the next morning, a pleasant young lady who delved straight to the issue at hand. She went through the case notes and called for the tests from the previous day. The blood tests returned with some questionable parameters. They showed a very high ESR. That was a term I had not paid much attention to earlier, so it was still new to me. Apparently the ESR blood test measures how quickly the red blood cells settle at the bottom of a test tube. A faster-than-normal rate obviously meant something was just not right.

The doctors continued to run more tests and placed her on yet another cocktail of intravenous antibiotics. It appeared the blood transfusion that sparked up the energy was waning, as low energy returned by day two, and it progressively went downhill. Innomama could no longer walk. She could only pass urine but could not poop. Her eyes were swollen, and the tale got worse each day.

Her dad and I became increasingly perturbed. Fear gripped us every now and again, but we stayed positive, praying and believing that everything would be all right. We tried to live a normal life in the hospital despite the challenges, but it was impossible. We had sleepless nights and had to be alert and vigilant. On one occasion, a nurse was on the verge of administering a wrong dose of medication, but we intercepted immediately, applying our knowledge from the earlier hospital stay to avert the situation.

So many people stood by us and showered us with love while in Lagos. The support was amazing. Calls poured in from family, friends, colleagues, bosses and church members. The managing director of the company Tobin worked for visited, which we found very humbling. Further tests confirmed that Innomama's blood count had dipped and was at the lowest since the journey started. Lilian, a friend and colleague, visited us at the hospital. She brought pumpkin leaves, salt, and made some pumpkin juice, all of which were considered useful in restoring the blood to normal levels. At this point, we valued every option we were given.

They had exhausted all tests, in our opinion, when the paediatrician suspected it might be juvenile arthritis and proposed to run a test to affirm or refute it. Interestingly, my immediate elder brother, Neji, and younger sister Mbong are both medical doctors and were following up on the case closely. Mbong, who was undergoing psychiatry specialist training in Lagos, hinted that from the medical results we had shared, it was a terrible infection or a malignancy. My brother was practising as a family doctor, and he tended to agree. They drew these preliminary conclusions from Innomama's extremely elevated ESR values. The last thing I wanted to deal with or accept was something as dreadful as a malignancy, so we stayed focused and positive.

We'd spent roughly a week in the hospital when the final test was done to rule out juvenile arthritis. The shocking news after a nurse drew blood for the test was that we had to wait ten more days for results. Apparently, no laboratory in Nigeria could run the test, so samples had to go to South Africa. This information took us unawares, and we wondered how best to manage the wait. Several questions spiralled in my head: *What next? How does one manage the ever-dropping blood levels? Sit and watch for the next ten days or move?* Movement seemed the most sensible thing to do.

I approached the senior consultant in the hospital for a formal debrief, and when the story wasn't much different, I requested that a note be prepared to my employers that stated clearly their inability to get the diagnosis right and the need to have Innomama referred to another medical facility. The doctor was not comfortable to let us go. He still believed it was a tough strain of malaria not yet traced. He encouraged me to stay back and wait for the tests results while they continue with antibiotics and any other process considered helpful. In his words, 'Be positive. The child's condition has improved'.

If this had happened anytime in 2018, I probably would have said, 'Like, seriously?', as that seemed to be the common response to ridiculous statements. At the time, I simply gave him a brief lecture. I made it clear he could not be more positive than I, the mother who waited almost five years to have the child. I also reminded him that the child, who was no longer walking or eating and was now barely talking, was unlike the happy girl who walked into his consultation room the first day we arrived at the clinic. How possible is it that the child had improved? When did he plan to admit there was no progress? Those reminders made him succumb and send my employers the letter and prepare a note for the next set of doctors we would likely consult.

The next question was where to? There were some travel restrictions for health-related trips linked to cost optimisation initiatives in my organisation, and my employers could only refer cases to South Africa or France if they considered it an emergency that needed foreign intervention. Unfortunately, my French visa wasn't valid, and I didn't have a visa to go to South Africa. It so happened that both countries had stopped granting expedited visas, and we needed a minimum of three weeks to get one. Given Innomama's condition, that luxury of time did not exist. I only had a valid United States visa, and thankfully, my employers were kind enough to approve my trip with a three-week view.

CHAPTER SIX

Stepping Out of Our Comfort Zone

There was a red polka-dot top and red jersey trousers Innomama owned that had a way of making her look bright and cheery. We thought it was the most perfect outfit till she wore it on 20 June, 2008, and we struggled to find any trace of that cheer. She had an incessant fever, was weak, and could not eat or walk. Her eyes were swollen and her face so pale that she looked a shadow of herself. As we checked out of the company's guest house and headed for the airport, carrying Innomama on my shoulders while her dad managed the luggage, I felt totally helpless.

It was a day of mixed feelings. We needed to get going; a diagnosis was necessary. The journey ahead was unclear, the outcomes unknown, but we had to do what we had to do bravely! A party of four started off to Lagos: dad, mum, Innomama and the unborn child, but soon enough, the search party would dwindle to three. It was a tough decision on whether the whole family should travel or not. I suggested that I go alone as the forerunner. Tobin pushed back but eventually saw reason with me and agreed to stay back in Nigeria.

It was an uneventful ride to the Murtala Mohammed International Airport in a 14-seater bus with a few colleagues who were travelling out of the country as well, most of whom were oblivious to what we were dealing with as we struggled to exchange pleasantries. We waddled through the airport protocol, deep in thought, and barely talked to anyone other than those involved in the check-in process for our Delta Air Lines flight. This done, we were set to leave for Atlanta. This was an emotional time for me, as my husband and I were parting ways at an uncertain time. We had all been in it together, and I am not sure how he was processing it. Soon he was to return to an empty house, while the rest of us proceeded in the search for a solution to an awkward problem. We said our goodbyes and assured ourselves that all would go well.

We boarded the aircraft, and I was grateful that the airline assigned us a bulkhead seat for the 13-hour journey to Atlanta. Innomama's fever continued through the flight, and keeping food or liquids down was an impossible feat. Anxiety and frustration set in as I battled to administer Ibuprofen to get the fever under control, but I kept my mind on the goal while I struggled to find a workable solution. The passenger next to me observed the situation and offered to help.

Coincidentally, she was a nurse who practised in the United States and had visited her family in Nigeria briefly. She quickly came to my aid, applied pressure on Innomama's nostrils, which forced her to breathe through her mouth, and seized the opportunity to drop the medication down her throat. What a relief! I had resumed breastfeeding my 21-month-old daughter all over again soon after she took ill. I doubt any milk came out, but those moments meant she cuddled closely, somewhat a comfort for both of us. I guess my breast became her source of succour or, I should say, a pacifier during the trip. Slowly but surely, we kept pushing till we made it to Atlanta.

We arrived in Atlanta safely on the evening of 20 June, 2008, a date that remains ever fresh in my memory. My elder brother, Tambu, was right there at the airport to pick us up. I am certain he struggled with recognising the niece he had seen barely three months earlier. We hugged each other, and he assured us everything would be just fine. He drove us straight to the emergency unit of

Children's Healthcare of Atlanta, Scottish Rite hospital. We pulled up to the valet parking and experienced first-class service right from the entrance. They attended to us promptly, taking Innomama's vital signs and immediately placing her on a medication to keep the fever under control.

Though we handed over the medical letter from the hospital in Nigeria to the team on duty, they were more interested in getting a history directly from me. So, the questioning session began. I poured out all the history I had up to that time to the best of my ability, even as I struggled with the medical terminology I had picked up from previous hospital visits.

When they'd gathered all the necessary information, they ordered many other tests, mainly from the radiology department. I was used to X-rays and ultrasounds, but this time around they also ordered a CT scan (Computerised Tomography) and MRI (Magnetic Resonance Imaging). These tests were new to me, so it was my turn to do the questioning and internet research. A CT scan is still an X-ray but a more detailed one that involves taking a series of images from different angles to create cross-sectional images of the bones, blood vessels and other parts inside the body. The MRI uses a large magnet and radio waves to look at organs and structures inside the body, from torn ligaments to tumours, to the brain and the spinal cord.

I was exhausted from the trip, but I had to complete the paperwork. I did not have any medical insurance, so they referred me to the financial counsellor. Without mincing words, I stated I was going to be a self-pay patient. This was on the back of medical bills for myself and dependents being comprehensively covered by my employer. She advised that I revert if I had any issues on financing down the road, which I reluctantly acknowledged.

They allocated Innomama a room in the hospital, which we moved into immediately. The bed was big enough for both of us, which was comforting after the 13-hour flight. My brother stayed with us until midnight. The hospital's cooling system was comparable to a freezer, given that we had just left a very humid environment. Carving out a coping mechanism was just not working. I had only travelled from Nigeria with four pieces of clothing, and nothing in our luggage resembled a sweater or blanket. I did not hesitate to cry out for help. They handed us some warm and toasty hospital blankets. It was heavenly. I never knew there was anything such as a blanket warmer—yet another first for me. Sadly, the feeling was short-lived; the blankets soon became cold and not much help after all.

I struggled through the night, turned, tossed, curled up, but I just could not find a comfortable position. It had been over a month since I left the comfort of my bed and moved from one clinic to the other. I thought I had mastered the act of sleeping in clinics, but here I was battling a new aspect: cold. I survived the night with Innomama cuddled next to me. She turned to breastfeeding frequently for comfort, a pacifier in human form. I finally fell asleep, one baby in my tummy and another on my breast.

The next day was a Saturday with numerous tests lined up. After the early morning grooming routine, a nurse came to get us for the scheduled tests. I noticed that everyone who came into the room wore a disposable cover over their scrubs. It mattered little to me, as I thought it was the norm. It was not till we stepped out of the room for the first time that I realised they had cordoned us off or more like had a sign that warranted extra caution in dealing with us. The inquisitive part of me sprang up, and the nurse explained that since we had come in from a tropical region with no diagnosis, they needed to take precautions just in case we had any communicable diseases.

Innomama was weak and could not even walk. I did a lot of shoulder-carrying prior to this but got introduced to a new friend, a buggy on four wheels. It was so helpful and practical for navigating the hospital. My shoulder could finally take a break. The CT scan, MRI and blood draw took roughly two hours but happened in quick succession, after which we returned to our room.

The catchy phrase 'health is wealth' is commonly used, but how well understood is it? I think it becomes real as you walk down the hallway of a hospital as a visitor, patient, guardian or parent. Your heart literally stops beating for a second! Scottish Rite hospital could easily be compared to a five-star hotel by any standard. It was beautiful, clean, cold, gadget-filled and had very warm staff, but it was not exactly where anyone wanted to be. There would always be a case better than yours, worse than yours, or just hopeless. Deep breaths amidst gratitude became a constant within such a brief span. We survived that day with all its attendant highs and lows.

The next day was a new day and a hope-filled one at that. It was a Sunday morning. I had prayed, made my confessions, and had my headphones on as I listened to worship music. We were expecting the test results and maybe finally a diagnosis.

When a doctor walked into the room, cheery and full of positive energy, my heart lit up. She announced that the preliminary results of some tests were indicative of a very serious bone infection. To allay any fears I might have, she said we would need about six weeks for the treatment but assured me everything would be just fine. There was, however, a 'but' in the story line. She explained that the pictures from the MRI had a peculiar characteristic that looked like thick glue, especially on the limbs. They needed further tests to determine what it could be; only then could the diagnosis be complete and treatment options started. The doctor left me thinking a six-week course of treatment was longer than expected but promising. At least there was some light at the end of the tunnel, or so I thought.

They ordered an MIBG scan for further checks. This took me back to my internet research route again. MIBG is an acronym for metaiodobenzylguanidine, a word I struggled to pronounce. We were now headed toward nuclear medicine. It involved injecting a radioactive dye into the system and subsequently scanning to check how the tracer attaches to some cells. This was used to confirm certain tumour types, one of which was linked to the nervous system. It was roughly a 45-minute scan. The patient needed to be relatively still for most of those scans. Where this could not be achieved, the patient might require anaesthesia. I had observed from the previous day that most of the scanning machines had video screens attached to them that helped keep children distracted during lengthy procedures. Innomama could watch an episode of *Barney*, a kids' programme, and stay still enough during the scan. Moreover, she was too weak to be boisterous.

After the scans, we spent most of the time lying down. I am uncertain if it was fatigue, jet lag or just me deep in thoughts. It was now obvious it was not a contagious ailment, and though there were no restrictions, the room seemed a safe space for the state of my mind. Nurses kept checking on

Innomama to ensure her temperature was under control. They also made it a point of duty to check her oxygen level and blood pressure each time they stopped by. For someone who wasn't comfortable around strangers, Innomama was relatively calm and cooperative. The nurses were warm and kind. They never hesitated to give an update when asked. I was eager to know what the results were, but only a doctor could provide that information.

I was told by one of the nurses that a doctor was coming to see her later that day. I expected the doctor who stopped by earlier to show up again, but alas, this time it was a different doctor. She was an African American doctor with dreadlocks. It was usual to break the ice and ensure the patient or guardian was in a good place and coping well before progressing to other discussions. We observed all that protocol prior to the principal business. As soon as she asked if I had family around or anyone who could be present so we could discuss the diagnosis, I immediately sensed there was more to it. I was eventually informed that further tests revealed it was one of the childhood cancers: neuroblastoma. Goose bumps covered my body!

What? Cancer? Neuro-what? How? Where from? I was transfixed momentarily. Cancer was the last thing on my mind. How on earth can a child that young be dealing with cancer? The questions did not stop popping up in my head. I was so confused that I even tried to let her know that the earlier doctor said it was a bone infection, blah, blah, blah. But of course that was me seeking the solace that did not exist. The diagnosis was definite this time. I was broken and could not hold back my tears. I hugged my daughter tightly. She must have wondered what was going on. I wasn't sure how or who to break the devastating news to. Shortly after, while the doctor waited for me to process the information, my phone rang. It was her dad.

Amidst sobs, I broke the news to Tobin. He asked for details, but I was not in the right state of mind, nor could I even pronounce neuroblastoma.

It was tough for him to fathom. He asked questions that I could not answer. He offered to come immediately, but I discouraged him, as the picture of the journey ahead was still unclear. He tried to stay as calm as he could manage from a distance. Given the subject, Innomama, was right there, we had to take hold of ourselves, pray to God and remind ourselves of His faithfulness. My brother showed up soon after and stayed long enough to ensure I sufficiently calmed down.

After the shock and attendant hysterical response, it was time to swing into action. They needed a discussion with us to outline the treatment protocol and strongly recommended that a family member who could digest all the information be present. As can be imagined, I was like someone in a trance. Naturally, my go-to family member had to be Tambu. An appointment was fixed for Monday, 23 June, 2008.

Just when we were getting used to the medical personnel in the wing we were initially admitted into, we were required to move to the Aflac Cancer and Blood Disorders Center, the cancer treatment wing of Children's Healthcare of Atlanta, following the confirmed diagnosis. With each move, it became more of a reality than a trance. Paediatric cancer stared us in the face. I wasn't sure what to expect in a cancer wing, but soon after we met extremely warm staff at the Aflac Center. They were welcoming and ready to make us feel at home—that is, if a hospital can ever feel like home. Their attitude lightened the burden.

We gathered with the medical team at a gigantic table in a conference room, my brother seated next to me. We were ready to hear and understand what was going on. Upon establishing our presence of mind, the doctor reminded us of the diagnosis. He started off with a brief history of paediatric cancers, including neuroblastoma, and the fact that the root cause was still uncertain, though studies were ongoing. He ran us through the results of the scans from the last two days. The primary site of the cancer was the right adrenal gland, but cancerous cells had spread out from the mass located there. They found traces in the bone marrow, scalp and eye region. As terrifying as it seemed, we were lucky that the cancer had not invaded the brain or eyes. It had spread so much that they classified it as Stage 4 cancer!

While I tried to situate myself, he outlined the treatment protocol, which would involve a surgery to excise the mass, six cycles of chemotherapy, two stem cell transplants, radiation therapy and six months of Accutane. The medical jargon made my head swim. They gave us an opportunity to ask questions. We were interested in the side effects, prognosis, past successes and much more. The duration of the treatment was a key element, which we were told would be anywhere between 12 and 18 months.

At some point I was physically present, but my spirit had left the room. Comprehending the whole thing was a tough call. I struggled to believe that I heard right; I struggled to believe it was happening to us, and I could not hold back the tears that dripped uncontrollably from my eyes.

Confusion reigned in my entire being: the fears, the options, the future, the feeling of hopelessness, the constant reminder of the baby in my tummy... and my sweet little 21-month-old Innomama. The emotions were mixed and running wild; I was broken yet again. My brother tried to remain strong and consoled me, though I suspect he was attempting to calm himself as well. It was hard to take it in, so the medical personnel paused, which helped me come to terms with my new reality.

As dampening as the news was, the doctors did their best to explain empathetically and offered limited assurances, though my assimilation was poor and vision blurred.

CHAPTER SEVEN

The Bumpy Adventure Begins

I have heard it said that crises are opportunities disguised in work clothes. How did we attempt to navigate the terrain in this instance? The Word. Yes, the Word of God. That was our only anchor and source of strength. I recall leaving Port Harcourt with a friend's portable CD player. My favourite song of faith, which I had held on to even when the diagnosis was unknown, had lyrics that seemed to jump out verbatim from scripture in Jeremiah 32:17: 'Ah Lord God, thou hast made the heavens and the earth by thy great power ... Nothing is too hard for thee'. That was my word for the season – nothing was too difficult for God. It was time to brace up and trust Him.

It was the usual practice to have the patient's name on the door of the hospital room for identification. The nurses had prepared a label with her first name, Innomama, and had it inserted when the room got allocated. I requested that they change it to her middle name, Osunyameye. They asked me why, and my response was simple: it is her name. I needed that constant declaration over her life and the reminder that nothing is impossible with God. It was difficult for the medical personnel to pronounce. They requested a shortened version, and I offered that they use Onsu. They updated the identification tag, and everyone complied.

Her surgery was scheduled for 25 June, 2008, five days after we arrived from Nigeria. This involved assessing the primary site where the cancer started from and excising the mass. Many of the medical personnel at Aflac were drawn to Innomama and sought to know more about her. They referred to her as the polite girl from Nigeria because she never failed to make a request without using the magic word *please*.

The oncologists and a few nurses had mentioned there was a Nigerian who was doing her fellowship with the Aflac team. They promised to look out for her and get us connected as soon as possible. I looked forward to the opportunity of having a Nigerian in my corner, someone who could walk with us through the uncharted path ahead.

A day before the surgery, while Onsu and I lay on the bed, there was a tap on the door. I imagined it was a medical technician who must have come over for the regular vital signs check. When I turned over, I realised the visitor did not have scrubs on. With a familiar accent, she introduced herself as Fola Adisa. The medical team had contacted her, and she stopped by to offer some moral support. As we spoke, it was obvious they had given her the full dossier on the pregnant Nigerian mother with a polite 21-month-old diagnosed with cancer.

I recall she had on a white-and-black dress, with her hair nicely blow-dried. Interestingly, she was pregnant too. That was how our paths crossed. It was an opportunity to ask some more questions and prepare myself psychologically for the tasks ahead. She answered all my questions to the best of her ability, causing no fear as she could relate with the faith journey we were embarking on.

The day of the surgery came so fast. They put me through the entire process via a long lecture of the procedure, anaesthesia, the expected outcome, risks and much more. The doctors were positive the procedure would go well, but all the same, it was important to explain the risks and get parental consent, which I gave. What other choice did I have? Throughout the process, I gave her dad the step-by-step updates. He could only visualise what was going on in his mind's eye because video calls with our phones were not common. Knowing God was not limited by distance, we prayed over the phone and encouraged each other in the Lord. They rolled Innomama into the theatre and advised on how long the surgery would likely take. I could only gaze upwards, immerse myself in prayer and trust God to take charge.

I returned to the room and shuttled back and forth till I could get an update. Hours later, she was rolled out of the theatre and back to the room. The surgeon gave me a debriefing almost immediately. They had successfully excised the mass from her adrenal gland, damaging none of her organs. That in itself was worth being thankful for. They had also taken the opportunity to insert a port into the upper left side of her chest. The port is an implantable device placed under the skin and used to draw blood and give intravenous fluids. It is especially useful for paediatric oncology practice. This was meant to remain inserted throughout the treatment regime, for the chemotherapy, and they would route blood draws through the port to prevent poking her each time she needed to take a course of treatment. They lectured me on how to maintain excellent hygiene for Onsu, especially at bath time. The precaution helped prevent infections which could lengthen the treatment time, lead to another surgical process or even be fatal.

She came out looking frail, but we were happy to be headed in the right direction.

***

In life, even when you think you know what to expect, you can never really understand it in its entirety till you experience it. The kickoff – or maybe the 'kick in' – of chemotherapy was one such experience for me.

Onsu had to go through six cycles of chemotherapy, each lasting five days, at intervals ranging from three weeks to one month. She started off with the first cycle barely four days after the surgery, and they briefed me on what to expect: nausea, loss of appetite, hair loss, extremely low blood counts... the list goes on. I had never seen chemo administered, so I was a bit uncertain and could only imagine what the actual reaction would be.

I heard a tap at the door, and a nurse practitioner stepped in with a little bag that looked like an intravenous solution. She introduced herself, explained her mission, shared the name of the drug with me, and confirmed she was in the right room and with the right patient by checking that the details on Innomama's wristband corresponded with those on the medication.

The process of administering the drip was painless. Considering the port had already been inserted, it required no direct skin poking, and for that I was thankful. Day one went well. The medical technicians constantly checked her vital signs, and they were all okay. Innomama experienced light nausea here and there but not as severe as they had initially made it sound, or so I thought.

Cycle one ended, and it was time to be discharged after spending the first two weeks in the hospital. Chemotherapy takes a toll on the blood cells and really crashes them. The body needs to recover and the blood cells return to a reasonable level before starting another cycle. Innomama needed injectable shots daily to help this process, especially building up the white blood cells quickly enough for the next cycle. The hospital had the shots dropped off at Tambu's home within 48 hours. A nurse would visit to give her the shots daily, and they required us to return to the clinic often to check how the blood cells were picking up. Part of the discharge instructions was a warning to ensure I rushed her to the hospital if her temperature ever got to 38.3 degrees centigrade. Chemotherapy compromises the immune system, and there was no room for infections. To buttress the point further, they gave us a laminated card that read, 'Her name is Innomama Dickson. She is a cancer patient and must be treated as an emergency if her temperature gets to 38.3 degrees centigrade'. There were numbers to call on the card as well. That card granted her priority treatment if she ever needed to be rushed to the hospital at brief notice.

There was a remarkable improvement right after the first cycle. Innomama could walk around quite easily with less pain, so my shoulders took a break and I was in high spirits. She was so glad to be home with her favourite cousin, Ata. I am teary as I write this portion. They were so close and played well together each time they had an opportunity. Ata, being a boy, played with such abandon that it tested my patience and perseverance levels. They could finally continue their play from where they stopped earlier in March 2008, though Innomama's strength was yet to return fully.

Now home after the first cycle, all the predicted symptoms played out one after another. She just couldn't keep any food down. Throwing up became the alternative lifestyle, and cleaning up after she puked followed suit. Her hair gradually started thinning out. She got tired and weak easily but was coping as best as she could. I struggled to come to terms with the changes I witnessed.

The nurse showed up for a few days, as I was expected to give her the shots afterwards. It was a very thin needle, but let's be real; even the tiniest needles hurt, don't they? The shots had to be given on her thighs for seven to 14 days. The nurse watched me manage a session and subsequently handed over the process to me. I had to hold her down each day at 6pm to practice my newly acquired nursing skill. She would scream like a huge nail was being passed through her skin, but I had no choice but to be strong, do it and get the spot dressed neatly to minimise the bleeding. With each passing day, it became more bearable.

Logistics for hospital appointments, however, remained an enormous challenge. The appointment times were not favourable enough for my brother to take us each time. He was an employee, and even though he was absolutely willing to help, it sometimes put a lot of pressure on him, as the commute to and from the hospital took from one to three hours, depending on traffic. I had not found myself so dependent in a long time, and it bothered me to have my brother inconvenienced as such.

While still recovering from the first cycle, I received the initial medical bill. The amount on it made my eyes pop. It became clearer why I was asked to see a financial counsellor from the word go. I didn't want my records tainted. I had always paid my bills. Even when I gave birth to Onsu and the hospital offered an application for a funding scheme since I did not have a medical insurance, I turned it down. I did not want any official barring me from getting into the US because of unpaid bills or usage of citizens' privileges. With this bill, the Bible verse that came to mind was a portion of Ecclesiastes 10:10, which states: 'Wisdom is profitable to direct'. If two weeks of treatment cost this much, and we had almost a year's treatment to go, how were we going to cope?

Immediately, I recalled the financial counsellor's advice: 'I understand you not wanting your records messed up; however, the financial help is not for you but for your daughter who, by the way, is an American citizen. It is her entitlement.' Those words became true to me in that instant. I was certain my employers would struggle to accommodate those bills; medical bills from America were not within the range they covered in the first place. I only found myself in America strictly by plans orchestrated by God. My husband and I couldn't afford those bills either, as they were astronomically high.

I looked for the financial counsellor's number and scheduled an appointment that aligned with the next hospital visit. Subsequently, we had a discussion around my needs and filled out all the forms required for processing the medical assistance. At that point, all I could do was pray for a positive response, as being stranded or turned back for my inability to foot the bills was not an option.

Soon, Onsu's blood cells picked up, and it was time to return to the hospital for the second cycle.

CHAPTER EIGHT

You Are Never the First

Having spent two straight weeks at the hospital, it had become familiar ground to us. I became less apprehensive as time to return for the next cycle of chemotherapy came closer. Between some of the interesting spots we had discovered and budding relationships and friendships, I had a few positive things to look forward to amidst the trials.

Hilda Manyo Dickson

We had acquaintances from our first stay, parents going through similar challenges with so many uncertainties. Three out of the many patients we met at the time had been diagnosed with neuroblastoma. Onsu was the youngest at 21 months; others ranged from four to eight years old. Just seeing them every now and again had a therapeutic effect on me.

The finest people I dealt with daily were the medical personnel. From the doctor assigned to Onsu's case, to the nurse practitioners, to the nurses and medical technicians, everyone was willing to help. It was simply amazing. After going through a couple of hospitals back home in Nigeria and the quality of service I received in some places, other than the industrial clinic in my office, it is no surprise that I found this facility and its staff so impressive. Every single one of them had something to offer; they tried to make me feel at peace by keeping me up to date with all the information about the diagnosis and coping with the process. They were never tired of answering questions. When anyone was uncertain, they directed me to someone who could provide an answer. When one of the medical technicians realised I didn't know about the perks available to me, like the kitchenette that had a lot of free supplies—cookies, tea, coffee, bread and other things that could make for a bearable hospital stay—she took time to educate me on how things worked around there. I noticed that there was no irritability in dealing with patients. We called as often as we needed to, and there was always someone willing to come with a cheerful smile. I'm not sure what the driver of their positive attitude was: the training, exposure, emoluments or the lucrative nature of the job, or maybe just a sense of fulfilment in playing a part towards healing of sick people? Whatever it was, I was glad for it. The thought of returning for the next cycle became somewhat bearable, though I couldn't wait to get Onsu's treatment over and done with. I had some control over my emotions, and part of this was because of the professionalism I experienced during our first stay.

***

They scheduled the next five days of chemotherapy with a fresh set of drugs, and the recuperating process was expected to follow a similar pattern. At this point I discovered that a patient could get platelets transfused too. I had only heard of blood transfusions prior to this, not broken-down components. I was learning a whole lot of new things and terminologies. I was in unfamiliar terrain and had become a mini researcher. I needed to understand and be in sync with what was going on. Google became my friend.

They had assigned a hospital room as usual, with the name Onsu on the door. The declaration and confession had to be a constant part of her journey. Each time they called her name, I unconsciously completed it by echoing,

'Osunyameye, nothing is impossible with God', a constant reminder and faith builder.

By the second cycle, it was time for deeper connections with the humans and environment: know the nurses better, connect with other families in similar circumstances, discover the hospital and just live in the moment, knowing full well who had the future. It was obvious we were not in it alone. So, with time, talking and laughing became much easier and coping strategies improved.

The second cycle was pivotal in the entire treatment regime, as I was made to understand. The treatment protocol was such that after the first two cycles of chemotherapy, she would require stem cell harvesting. The harvested stem cells would be stored for two transplant procedures scheduled to happen after the sixth chemo cycle. It therefore meant that the blood sample test after the second cycle must reveal the absence of 'bad cells'. In other words, the blood sample had to be free of cancer cells.

After dealing with the side effects of the first cycle at home, I realised I needed to speak to the chemotherapy drugs. You might wonder what it means to 'speak' to a drug; however, I took my Bible reference from Mark 11:23 which says, 'For assuredly I say to you, whoever says to this mountain, be removed and cast into the sea and does not doubt in his heart but believes that those things which he says will be done, he will have whatever he says'. Chemotherapy, though required for the treatment, was equally harmful to body cells and had several side effects, so I opined it was not out of place to have it classified as a mountain that I needed to speak to.

I doubt any of the nurse practitioners will forget us so easily, because each time they came into the room with the chemotherapy solution I would ask them to pause, and then I would speak to it and pray over the solution before administration. I always started off by saying, 'This chemotherapy will go in like water. It cleanses the system, destroys only the bad cells, has no business with the good cells and does not cause any side effect but only treats for good. In Jesus's name. Amen'. I said the same prayer each time the nurses walked in with the drugs, to the point that they began to learn it themselves. In one instance, the planned medication had strong reactive abilities with unpleasant side effects, and in acknowledging that my declarations might work, one practitioner stepped in with the solution and said together with me, 'This chemotherapy solution goes in like water…'. I completed the prayer and we both chuckled.

***

As Izaak Walton'once said, *'Good company in a journey makes the way seem shorter'*. It is arduous enough to walk an uncharted road, let alone companionless. I connected with exceptional people I met upon my path, fellow travellers en route to the same destination of recovery and kind helpers that gave support upon the way.

Dr. Adisa checked on us every now and again, which was particularly helpful. She encouraged us and was a positive part of our journey. She was one of the few who could relate to my Christian faith and my two-pronged approach of going through with the medical treatment for cancer but backing it up with the scriptural belief.

I learned through the nurses that a Ghanaian family had a son who had gone through the same journey a year or two earlier and showed up at the hospital for medical checks from time to time. I was excited to meet a fellow African who had walked this path. I was eager to know about their experience and how they coped with it. I requested to get their details so I could reach out. The financial counsellor contacted Constance, the child's mother, and thankfully she was willing to speak with me. With her permission, they shared her number, and I put a call through to her.

Constance was a cheerful lady, and we connected easily because beyond both of us being originally of African descent, my husband's late dad was a Ghanaian as well. Fortunately, she had a hospital appointment scheduled for her son and promised to pop into the Aflac Center to see us. True to her word, she visited us shortly afterwards with her son. My heart leapt for joy as soon as I saw him; there was hope! He was visibly doing well. She shared their story, from the first cycle of chemotherapy to the sixth, the two transplants and radiation afterwards. All I could say was, what a journey! She recommended a meal supplement, PediaSure, which she used for her son. Onsu could not keep food down after the first chemotherapy session, which was quite bothersome. That welcome tip and experience-sharing was very useful and somewhat comforting.

I got to meet Amanda as well, Joshua's mum. Joshua was a charming four-year-old who loved playing with toy cars. He was diagnosed with neuroblastoma too. Their hospital room was a couple of doors down from ours, and they were a friendly family. Amanda found Onsu adorable, as her smile was infectious. We got to talk every now and again, exchanging tips and experiences as we went along. There was also an eight-year-old with neuroblastoma and many other kids with different forms of cancer. The Aflac Center dealt with different types of malignancies affecting various parts and organs in the body.

As I met different parents and had varied discussions, one question I could not find an answer to and still struggle with is what causes cancer in little children. If it is said that lifestyle was responsible for certain cancers in people, what could have led to such an ailment in children so young that they have barely lived, let alone have an identifiable lifestyle? I wondered if could it be attributed to a dormant genetic strain, like albinism, which abruptly appears down the generational line? Or was it perhaps owing to one or more unknown deficiencies from a parent, or both, or their combination? Or could the reason possibly lie deeper, in the spiritual, as was with the man from Siloam who was born blind so that the works of God might be displayed in him? I couldn't tell.

***

You could get really bogged down and bored in an enclosed hospital room, which meant needing to stretch out now and then to remain sane. We discovered the garden just at the corner of the chapel, well-kept with lovely flowers, seating areas and a little fountain with some coins probably dropped in by people who had several wishes. I could relate to that.

The hospital's lobby was a sight to behold. Plaques honouring those who had given funds towards building the hospital were displayed on the wall on both sides of an enormous aquarium. Watching the wide variety of beautiful, multicoloured fish was a favourite pastime for Onsu. She found them fascinating, and with the ease of navigation created by the buggy, we could linger there a bit before we moved along on our tour of the hospital, enjoying the sights and sounds of our environment.

There was also a lovely gift shop in the lobby and a café with a wide variety of sandwiches. I had gotten hooked on hot chocolate milk there before I discovered the free goodies station on the admissions floor, though the sandwiches remained a go-to each time I was not in the mood for a typical hospital meal. Each relationship and discovery played a part in distracting me from the gruelling experience of cancer. In various ways, they helped Onsu and I cope with our ordeal. They provided a sense of normalcy that improved our experience together as mother and child, which in turn enabled us to connect and interact better with others. The entire hospital setting seemed like a carefully prepared garden soil that encouraged the seeds of hope and confidence to take root and grow.

***

The second cycle of chemotherapy went well, and we were back to the waiting game. Onsu was released and back at home for recovery. She still felt the effects of the drugs. Her hair continued falling out, and the nausea didn't cease, but we kept moving forward; we refused to be shortsighted. I updated Onsu's wardrobe to include some hats and trendy face caps. When she wasn't in some form of discomfort, you could trust her to beam with smiles, which always lit up the space and made her an attraction to many people.

I had advanced my skills in holding Innomama down prior to receiving her shots. The checks got slightly manageable as well after we discovered Children's Healthcare of Atlanta's Urgent Care/Outpatient Center in the same county where we lived. That was a lifesaver. The logistics became easier to cope with since most of the frequently required blood tests were conducted there and thus saved us trips to Scottish Rite, which was farther away. What a relief!

All this happened through integrating, communicating and exchange of ideas with fellow patients, medical personnel and the various angels God sent our way.

***

The medical team scheduled the stem cell harvest to take place right after the recovery period of the second cycle. If found clean enough, the stem cells would be stored for the transplant sometime after the sixth cycle. As one can imagine, this cycle really meant a lot to all of us. The shots and checks continued till it was finally time to harvest the cells.

Harvesting was not a term I was familiar with in the medical sense. I could relate planting crops to harvesting, but the complete business of stem cell harvesting was exploratory in nature as far as I was concerned. The medical practitioners would always tell us what to expect, but my mind's eye continued to attempt some level of visualisation till the actual procedure took place. After the second cycle of chemo, we showed up at the urgent care two to three times a week to check Onsu's blood levels. The first three times we left with mixed feelings. The blood count was well below the levels required before we could proceed with the stem cell harvest. On the one hand, we were happy to spend a few more days at home; on the other, we wanted it to pick up so we could get the treatment protocol over and done with. Somewhere around the fifth trip to the urgent care, Onsu's blood counts stabilised, which was exciting for me. It was time for a new adventure.

They slated the harvesting to take place at Children's Healthcare of Atlanta–Egleston. The building stood on the same premises as the popular Emory Hospital. It was an outpatient procedure, though with medicine you never really know. We arrived on time and had clearly respected all the instructions given prior, which included administration of medication to boost production of stem cells. We were in a corner room, and the administrator explained everything about the procedure.

Thankfully, the harvesting was non-invasive and involved temporarily removing blood from the body, separating stem cells and returning the blood to the body afterwards. The medical personnel attached Onsu to an apheresis machine that acted like a sieve, filtering the stem cells from the blood. It went on for about four hours, and I longed to rest my head on a proper bed, as sitting for that long wasn't comfortable for a pregnant lady like me, though I was just approaching my second trimester. I waited it out and remember receiving a call from a family friend during the process, which acted as an excellent distraction. I was hopeful that the harvest would be free of unwanted cells to avoid a repeat of the procedure.

We checked into the hospital a few days later for the third cycle and got the delightful news that the harvested stem cells were indeed clean.

CHAPTER NINE

What Went Wrong?

The third cycle took the regular toll on us in the hospital. I was getting accustomed to the symptoms and coping with them as best as I possibly could while observing the recommended hygiene protocol. Hygiene is always a big deal when dealing with a suppressed immune system. Medical researchers link some fatalities to infections due to a compromised immune system, not cancer, per se. When I heard things like, 'Oh the poor child had a stomach bug and passed on',

I had no choice but to buckle down and get finicky about supposedly tiny details.

I learned so much in the course of the journey. I learned that it was safer to use the knuckles in pressing elevator buttons than the tip of your finger. I learned that it was safer to sneeze into your elbow than into your palms. It became second nature to look for a piece of tissue or use my elbow to open doors, as doorknobs carried a lot of germs, irrespective of how shiny the metal might look. In essence, I avoided touching public objects and surfaces with my hands, especially when those parts of my hands could eventually get in my eyes, mouth or nose. So yes, I learned a lot.

As we approached the end of the third cycle, we looked forward to moving out of the hospital. I was excited, as we were expecting Onsu's dad to visit from Nigeria. We eagerly anticipated a quick rise in the blood counts so we could have a delightful break and her dad could see her in good shape. Ada and Tambu had recently had a second child, and we were keen on participating in my niece's first birthday too; the cake, picture taking, party favours and all that goes with it would be a more interesting outing than just hospital trips.

All our wishes came true. Tobin visited and was excited to see Onsu doing so well. We made the trips to the urgent care together for follow-up blood tests, and there was a semblance of normalcy, doing things together as a family. Onsu enjoyed visits to the park with her dad, where the swings got her reeling with excitement. There were only so many fun things we could do because we did not want to risk exposing Onsu to an infection of any kind, but we appreciated the brief visit before Tobin had to go back to work.

Onsu still had one more fun thing to do before we returned to the hospital for the fourth cycle: her cousin's birthday party. It had been a while since I saw her in a proper party dress. I dug up a white dress with black polka-dots and a green satin sash for her, while I wore a black-and-white maternity dress to create a scheme. Ada chauffeured us to Kinkos, a photography studio in Babies "R" Us, where we took some pictures that I considered nice enough to upload to Facebook. Thereafter, we returned home to the cake and rice to mark the day and the end of the treatment break. We were excited; we created a priceless memory!

***

We checked into the hospital for the fourth cycle, feeling exhausted and excited at the same time. It was the usual routine that went by swiftly. Yet another cocktail of chemotherapy administered, which I continued to confess and speak over as I had in earlier sessions. When the cycle ended, we went home as usual and resumed managing the aftermath hoping the blood counts bounced back quickly.

I had built my faith in God up to a level where I only expected good. It kept me going so that even when things looked bad, I was comfortable confessing positive and great outcomes. It had become part of my DNA. I always had an inner witness that God would never leave or forsake me.

The assurance was so strong that I am certain many people might have imagined I needed a psychologist to assess my mental well-being.

Onsu's birthday was fast approaching, and we were in high spirits. Every day was momentous, so wrapping up a complete year could only be a major milestone. I owed all my gratitude to God for the opportunity to celebrate our daughter's second birthday and could not hide my joy.

Something wasn't right. Onsu hadn't been her usual self of late. She barely talked, refused to eat and had become lethargic. Her beautiful, warm smiles had practically vanished. Beyond these, however, she seemed fine, and we couldn't discern any other physical symptom that indicated an underlying illness. Even her body temperature was normal. Try as I might, I could not figure out what was wrong, but intuitively I sensed a problem, and I was uneasy.

I looked forward to the photoshoot scheduled with Flashes of Hope, an organisation that occasionally offered free professional photos to families going through serious health challenges in the hospital. May the good Lord bless all the individuals and organisations who dare to be creative in order to ensure they meet various needs. I mean, other than the phones that have turned us all into instant photographers, who would ever think of a professional photo shoot while dealing with a health challenge? Courtesy of Flashes of Hope, I have tangible memories of a journey once travelled.

On the day of the photo shoot, I was certain Onsu would get excited and give us a gigantic smile because she loved taking pictures. However, she had stopped interacting with everyone, including me. Also, she showed no interest in her outfit, so I kept it simple: a short-sleeved, hooded pink jacket, a coffee-brown pair of trousers and a matching brown pair of shoes. We were set to go. Her Aunty Ada drove us to the hospital where the photo shoot would take place. I waited for the magic moment when Onsu would break the silence; well, that was far-fetched. She neither stood nor smiled. It was now very obvious that the little, polite Miss Chatty, always smiling girl, was in no mood to socialise. She just wore a blank look. The nurses tried and even wondered if there was a change of circumstances in the family, which was not the case. All the cajoling yielded no result. I had no choice but to carry her on my lap and smile wide enough for both of us.

This went on for the next few days, and I got even more worried. She was still not talking, barely ate, and staring into space was her new normal. I called the hospital, and they advised I bring her in for proper assessment, as all I described was difficult to comprehend over the phone. It was now obvious that her second birthday was going to happen in the hospital.

We checked into the clinic, and the doctors were at a loss to understand what was going on. All her vital signs were perfect. They didn't quite expect the symptoms she was exhibiting and struggled in linking it up with the treatments they had exposed her to so far. I started off with a therapeutic approach, as advised by the doctors. I took her on walks around the hospital—the chapel, the wish fountain, garden, aquarium and all the familiar sites that should ordinarily stimulate her senses. They all yielded no impressive result. The doctors decided to perform an electroencephalogram (EEG) to detect the electrical activity in her brain. That was a new medical term yet again. It involved having electrodes stuck at certain points on her head. The small metal discs were wired to a machine that read the activity in the brain. The results were all within normal parameters. Meanwhile, Onsu continued to stare in silence.

Now it was her second birthday, 12 September 2008, a day we had so looked forward to spending outside the hospital. But with her lacklustre disposition, I felt really sad for Onsu. Nevertheless, I wished I could turn things around for her sake and was determined to make the day count.

Aunty Ada ordered a lovely birthday cake. The nurses knew Onsu loved being a princess and were ready to make her one. They got her a princess party hat, a princess magic wand, a happy birthday sash and a card where they all dropped a note of encouragement. The package from the nurses was attractive and colourful, and I expected a magical smile to emanate out of the princess, but it didn't happen. We kept hope alive all the same. So many wishes came her way, but she just would not budge. It was great to hear the cheers and feel the love from all the nurses. It encouraged me and lifted my spirits.

At about 5.30pm, there was a knock on the door. It was her favourite cousin, Ata. To everyone's bewilderment, Onsu, who had not spoken for days, leaned forward to say her first and only word for her birthday: 'Ata'. We all jerked and were rather surprised. It was an answer to prayers. All attempts to get her to say more just did not work. That was it for the day, but then it was a confirmation that all was well. Now we could dig into the Thai rice Tambu and Ada had brought, along with the birthday cake. The birthday turned out great at the end. There was a glimmer of hope on the horizon. It was now obvious that familiar or favourite faces and places could help get Onsu to talk.

The next day I took Onsu to the little garden with the wish fountain. She brightened up there and even mumbled a thing or two. How exciting that was for me! She was on a journey to full recovery. Things got better and better each day till we got discharged. After that scary episode, I vowed never to stop her from being a chatterbox. We were never able to place our fingers on what went wrong.

The fifth and sixth cycles were less dramatic, thankfully. I continued to pray and speak over the chemotherapy, declaring it focused only on unhealthy cells.

The Word of God is power, and we were not about to stop believing in it!

CHAPTER TEN

All in the Mix for a Transplant

We always knew that they required two sets of stem cell transplants as part of the treatment protocol at Children's Healthcare of Atlanta. As we embarked on the journey, however, we became more aware of the damage the transplant process could leave on the body. I had asked if Onsu could have only one transplant done instead, but we were told we had to follow the hospital's protocol. All we needed was for our child to get well, so it was not so hard to say yes. There was no turning back, or so we thought, till an opportunity came up to join a study for a protocol of just one transplant session in the hospital. I quickly notified Tobin, and were we pleased? Exceedingly so. He encouraged me to opt for it and sign up. I was too excited to even ask what it entailed. We just knew that it reduced the treatment and recovery time by six to eight weeks, and we did not bother reading between the lines.

After the successful enrollment, I had no further updates on what to expect till Onsu suddenly got scheduled for a procedure that we felt was a bit invasive, given what she had dealt with prior. It involved an outpatient surgery to insert some tubes for passing medication, similar to the port she already had in her chest for chemotherapy. I enquired why they just could not continue with the port alone, and the response I got showed that she required it for the protocol we signed up for. I did not want her to go through any unnecessary procedure, as she had gone through a lot and looked frail to me. This limited my choices: either grant the consent required to insert the tubes, or Onsu was out of the study.

I had no peace! It was a tough decision to make; a second transplant session extending her treatment by over a month versus a 'simple' one-day procedure? I was not ready to take a chance, so I opted out and was back to the protocol of two transplants. My decision made little sense to me, but it came with peace. It felt like being denied a dream that already came true. We really wanted a single transplant, had prayed so hard for a shorter treatment span, but had to let the golden opportunity slip away because I had no peace.

The transplant had to happen right after the sixth chemo cycle. We needed a set of approvals from the government to go on with it. This was in year 2008. The recession had hit America and the world hard, and the election campaigns were on; the mix was just not right. Tobin had taken time off work to stay through the transplant, as the procedure required her to be hospitalised for at least one month. We were on standby for the next move that seemed to take forever.

***

My pregnancy had progressed significantly. I was in my third trimester, rolling along. My progress impressed the gynaecologist. I always left his clinic with a sigh of relief because the feedback was consistently good. My wardrobe needed an update, as winter was gradually creeping in and I don't cope well with cold. My tummy had tripled in size overnight, and I wondered how I was going to manage till the end of the hospital stay. I found it difficult to get a good night's rest. A comfy position on a soft mattress did not exist. It required more than an effort to pick things up from the floor. It occurred to me then that I had not bought the basic needs for the new baby. That was yet another worry to deal with. Thankfully, my husband was around, so it was easier to handle Onsu and start some shopping too.

I thought it wise to have my maternity bag all packed even before leaving for the month-long hospital stay. The shopping was a good idea and a welcome distraction. Each aisle popped with colour, especially those with things for baby girls, and joy emanated from within me. The mall was a good place to relieve tension while getting some much-needed physical exercise.

I was also studying for my professional exams. The plan was to take the ACCA Corporate Reporting exams (P2) from the United States to keep accounting concepts fresh for me. At that moment, I had many distractions and did not have to dwell endlessly on the approval for transplant. I was hell-bent on having some semblance of a balanced life amidst the awkward circumstance. Strange, right? Maybe, but it helped me stay sane and gave me a false sense of normalcy.

One cool afternoon while I lazed round, a call came through from Children's Healthcare of

Atlanta. I answered quickly, thinking it was time to check into the hospital. Instead, I was told that I needed to meet with the financial counsellor again. Disappointed and a bit confused, I set an appointment for the following day.

I sensed there must have been a problem with the transplant approval. What could it be? That got us concerned. Though we looked forward to getting the transplant done, were we physically, emotionally and mentally ready? That uncertainty lingered.

We set out to the hospital the next day to understand why we were called. In the course of our discussion, the financial counsellor said the economy was in recession, and the government's medical aid team quizzed the reason for two transplants, especially since there was no proof that two stem cell transplants had a better prognosis than one. In the end, the approval was granted for only one stem cell transplant. She gave us this news solemnly, almost apologetically. If she only knew! This was an answer to our prayers.

It had always been our desire to have just one transplant, so the decision was just one huge blessing in disguise for us. It was obvious that God had orchestrated the desired result.

***

The stem cell transplant process is extremely complicated. Simply put, it involves collecting and storing a patient's healthy stem cells, which was already done during the stem cell harvest referred to earlier. Thereafter, all the diseased blood cells are eradicated from the patient's body using a high dose of chemotherapy, and finally the stem cells are reintroduced into the body to start off the re-creation and restoration of new cells. So, as you might have rightly guessed, it is more or less a plug-and-play process, given that no organ was being removed from one person and donated to another. To make it easier, it was an autologous stem cell transplant, meaning Onsu's own healthy stem cells were being used, rather than those of someone else. The checklist had been fully ticked off, and we were ready for a smooth adventure.

We checked into Children's Healthcare of Atlanta—Egleston. Prior to this, we had been in Children's Healthcare of Atlanta—Scottish Rite, where we had discovered all the nooks and crannies. Egleston was an older hospital with different layout and new medical personnel. The protocol was different, so we needed to unlearn the protocols we were used to and learn how to function there. They did not allow visitors, and hygiene had to be at the highest level because of the compromised immune systems of all the children admitted in that section. The playroom remained highly regulated, with only children from the same household allowed at any given time.

The room assigned to Onsu was big enough for all three of us. I remember vividly that it was at the left corner at the end of the hallway. We went through the regular drill from the medical personnel prior to the treatment. Each drill always reminded me of the pregnancy book, *What to Expect When You're Expecting*. From the chemotherapy journey so far, it was obvious that one is never totally prepared for the arrival of an event till it comes. Everyone's experience, though similar, will depend on how they are wired. The good thing about it is that knowledge is power, so you are better off armed with some knowledge than going in totally unaware of what to expect.

The transplant process started almost immediately. Even after all the drills on what to expect, I had imagined my daughter would be hooked up to a machine like during the stem cell harvest, with blood flowing in and out of various tubes, but that was not the case. Onsu was hooked up to several devices to monitor her heart rate, oxygen level and other vital signs while the high-dose chemotherapy was issued just like the earlier doses of chemotherapy. Making positive confessions aloud over every medication before administration became our way of life again.

Onsu coped relatively well at the start. We thought we knew all there was to know about nausea till it set in shortly after the treatment began. We constantly had a bowl or waste collection bag with us, shuttling between the room and bathroom at frequent intervals. She was throwing up constantly, as if her internals were going through an intensive cleansing routine. The vomitus was clear, thick and gel-like. It was nothing like we had dealt with in the past.

The nurses continued to monitor her vitals often; the blood levels were at an all-time low, heading towards the expected zero level. You would think that would be scary enough, but the worst was yet to come. Onsu started retaining fluid about halfway into the treatment. She became swollen, and her complexion turned jet-black. Thankfully, her eyes remained open and clear. We could see she was in great agony, and even morphine didn't help. It was easier for me to bear since her dad was around, but it was a scary sight, I must confess. Other than pray and stay positive, there was absolutely nothing we could do. The doctors were also struggling to understand what was going on. We kept pressing on in prayers, doing our bit while being certain that God had it all in control.

In the earlier days of treatment, while at Scottish Rite, we could have her cuddled up in a buggy, take walks and just breathe. Here, we basically went nowhere for the duration of the treatment, as the last thing you wanted to deal with was catching a bug and complicating issues. It felt like being imprisoned.

We were rarely able to summon the courage to leave Onsu's side and go in search of food in the hospital's restaurant. Fortunately, there was a kitchen in the hospital that offered pre-made meals which we stored in the refrigerator. That came in handy so we could spend most of the time on our floor hunger-free with a variety of meals to feed on.

Thanksgiving Day, 27 November, 2008, was a reminder of all the blessings we take for granted.

You realise that the little things that matter are just within your reach if you would just open your eyes and heart to receive them. Some families took time out to bring food and gifts to those of us in the hospital. The nurses encouraged us to go down to the lobby to get some food. We did so reluctantly, as we had gotten used to staying on the admission floor and focusing only on our daughter. When we eventually got downstairs, we realised there were so many other families spending Thanksgiving in the hospital and dealing with distinct challenges. The buffet was all set, and there was already a long queue waiting to grab a meal. How thoughtful of the giving hearts!

What got us excited was the arts and crafts corner, which they set up to cater for young kids. We grabbed a T-shirt, inscribed Onsu's name on it and the meaning. We got a light meal and rushed up to the room to show her the new T-shirt. It cheered her up, even in her state. It was comforting.

We could hardly blink; sleep was far-fetched. Onsu's discomfort increased, and even the morphine pump that had been introduced to manage the pain brought little relief. Preparation for my professional exams took a back seat, as I could barely understand anything I tried to read. I ditched the idea of writing the exams and quickly advised the examination body.

Ultimately, the diseased blood cells were all destroyed, and the medical team introduced the stem cells. Voila! Transplant done. The wonders of God unravelled daily during this journey. Onsu's body accepted the stem cells, and over the next few days things slowly began to improve. Her dad had been around for about a month and needed to head back to Nigeria, as his time off work was up. He left reluctantly but with a better picture of where we stood midway through the process.

CHAPTER ELEVEN

Benevolence in Action

Post-transplant, the patient more or less is like a newborn baby that has never received a vaccination. The immune system becomes so compromised that it requires extra-special care every step of the way.

Our hospital stay was almost over, and though I looked forward to a break from it, I had genuine concerns. We needed accommodation in close proximity to the hospital, because Onsu would be required to come in daily for blood work and progress tests. The hour-long commute from Tambu's house would make that next to impossible. Tobin and I had explored various options but struggled to settle for one because of the various restrictions we had to deal with in managing Onsu.

Finally, it was time to be discharged from the hospital. We had strict protocols to adhere to. Onsu could not be around other children or even adults, and she could not go to public areas without a mask. Shopping with her was permitted only under exceptional circumstances but was best avoided. Social distancing was highly recommended. With all the dos and don'ts, going back to Tambu's house was really not an option. I didn't own a car to commute daily to the hospital, and there were children there. It just wouldn't work. Then, thanks to willing and giving hearts, we had an alternative: the Ronald McDonald House.

I was sceptical at first, despite the recommendations of hospital staff and families that had walked this path before us. I strongly believed it would just be another extension of the hospital. However, it appeared to be the only place that met all the conditions given by the hospital, so I signed up for that option. The Ronald McDonald House is a home away from home that brings hope to families in distressing situations. It was specially designed for families with extremely ill children or those with complex medical conditions who were getting treated miles away from home. They provide accommodation for a token, to ensure families are close enough to support each other rather than dealing with a separation during an already difficult time. Their houses are usually situated close to big or specialty hospitals to help bridge the accommodation gap.

The management of the Ronald McDonald House in Atlanta approved our stay, and we moved in there when we were discharged. To my utter amazement, it was far from what I expected it to be. It was exquisite and comely. Upon check-in, I realised they had regular rooms with attached bathrooms and some suites with kitchenettes. They dedicated the suites to patients who needed to be isolated due to compromised immune systems or other life-threatening conditions. The suite assigned to us could best be likened to a five-star apartment-hotel. It had a living room, a bedroom with two queen-sized beds, and a fully equipped kitchenette. It had either just undergone renovation or was newly built and was in excellent condition.

There was a common area where families that did not have so many restrictions could hang out, and a kitchen with every appliance you could think of. The pantry could pass for a supermarket; we could find any cooking supply or snacks we needed. They stocked the pantry courtesy of different giving hearts. Besides that, some families consistently brought cooked meals on certain days of the week. Though I cooked most of our meals, I could not help but admire the families that volunteered their time and resources to ensure they met the needs of others.

The manager and staff at the Ronald McDonald House, most of whom I learned were volunteers as well, were exceptionally polite and always willing to help. I could describe the entire ensemble as benevolence in action. I was so impressed and dreamt of replicating such a service someday, a dream I still hold close to my heart.

I really can't come this far without a special mention of Aunty Ify, a friend to my brother's family, who ended up being a go-to person God sent my way. Though she was dealing with several personal challenges, she always offered and showed willingness to assist each time I needed to do grocery shopping. She would take time out to drive us to Publix to get groceries or whatever else we might require. Most times, I could leave Onsu in the car with her to avoid exposure. She even went the extra mile to cook food and bring it over to us. For someone I had no prior relationship with, I found the gesture magnanimous.

***

Commuting to the hospital for Onsu's medical checks was so much easier from our new place. We only needed to make it to the pickup point and join the shuttle bus to the hospital and back daily. It made life so manageable, and public transport served when I had an appointment with the gynaecologist for my pregnancy checks. I also arranged with a cab driver I had used occasionally while at my brother's place to manage some aspects of my movements when I had no alternative. He was glad to be of help and picked me up at a discounted rate each time I needed his service.

With each visit to the hospital, Onsu's blood tests showed an upward trend, while the results from the medical checks kept getting better and better. We did not have to get readmitted for a fever or a stomach bug; for that we remained grateful. With Onsu's positive response to treatment and little or no nausea, my sleep pattern improved. Onsu could eventually interact a bit more when her blood count improved significantly. She returned to her cheerful self and never lost her smile. She smiled so much that she practically became a model. I even granted the manager of the Ronald McDonald House permission to take pictures of her for publicity.

I remained in contact with a few friends and acquaintances who were still undergoing treatment at Scottish Rite. A fellow mum had opted to try the antibody approach, which she felt would give her son a better chance at surviving the 'monster'. During our exchanges on how Onsu coped with the transplant process and how her son's treatments were going, she recommended I join the support group for neuroblastoma mums. What a great opportunity for knowing what others were doing, how they were coping with recoveries, life after treatment and much more, or so I thought. I envisaged the support group would be a great outlet for getting answers to lingering questions and closing some knowledge gaps.

I joined the group, and things took a whole unique twist. Throughout the cancer journey, I had never been as disturbed as I was barely two days after joining the support group. There was so much negative news about neuroblastoma that it robbed me of sleep. It was obvious the news had altered my eye and soul gates. The biblical principle that faith comes by hearing the Word of God is as true for fear; fear comes by hearing negative things. I remained shaken for some days, I must confess. I went back to sleepless nights and even had nightmares in the process.

I contacted Dr. Adisa and asked some strange questions that made her wonder what I was feeding on. She is a firm believer in Christ and immediately sensed I had messed with something new. When she probed further, I shared the experience of the support group. She immediately recommended I exit the group, which I had already done, but some damage had been inflicted. The overload of negative information messed up my faith so badly that I wondered why I made such a huge mistake. All things work together for a purpose, though, as that huge mistake birthed this book. There and then, I made a vow to write a book when my daughter pulled through the ordeal. I was convinced I needed to get some positive news out there, because it was lacking when I needed it. There is so much hope in Christ.

To reset my mind, I discovered Joel Osteen's services online and started feeding my soul with some good, positive stuff to wipe off the negativity. That was the birthing of online worship for me, back then in December 2008. I read only uplifting articles or books while listening to a lot of praise and worship songs. An exchange between negative and positive information took place in my mind, and I felt better after a couple of days.

Just as we spent Thanksgiving in the hospital, we also spent Christmas of 2008 at the Ronald McDonald House. The difference was that Onsu was out of the hospital, stronger and up on both legs. Her body, to a reasonable extent, had recovered from the battering of the last high dose of chemotherapy required prior to the transplant. The generation of new blood cells was well underway. Zero platelets and red blood cells were a thing of the past, and the numbers were picking up nicely. It was exciting to see things turn around.

People showed up yet again with meals and gifts for those who could not make it home for Christmas. Later that evening, Tambu stopped by to pick up Onsu and me to visit a family friend, the Obohos. He was accompanied by my other brother, Neji, who had flown in from Knoxville, Iowa, to spend the Christmas season with us in Atlanta. I did not realise how much we needed the change of scenery until we arrived at the Oboho's place. It was a vast house with many nooks and crannies to explore. The family offered us a variety of Nigerian food that took me back home for a moment, and during the meal we discussed refreshing topics that took my mind off our arduous journey. We returned to the Ronald McDonald House late that night and went straight to bed.

It was a glorious Christmas Day!

CHAPTER TWELVE

Getting Closer to the Finish Line

We had ticked the boxes for chemotherapy, a stem cell transplant, and it was now time for radiation therapy. The American Cancer Society explained the process as 'using high-energy particles or waves such as X-rays, gamma rays, electron beams or protons to destroy or damage cancer cells'.

I gathered that precision and accuracy were the key elements of radiation. Though other treatments, like chemotherapy, expose the entire body to cancer-fighting drugs, radiation is a local treatment that only targets the specific areas that need it. It has its own side effects, which is why it is key to focus only where the rays are required. No more, no less! Like most cancer treatment options, you struggle with weighing the benefits against the drawbacks.

The radiotherapy was scheduled to take place in Emory Hospital, which was in the same vicinity as Egleston, where the transplant took place. The clinic treated both adults and children, so that was a pattern change for us. As usual, we had to be at the hospital for an assessment and debrief. The radiation oncologist informed us of the plan to have radiation on her head region as well as the primary site of the cancer, the adrenal gland. She required the radiation at those spots to inhibit any further growth, while acknowledging that it could cause other cancers. Our dilemma was clear, but we had to keep moving forward.

I did not think the head region needed radiation, going by the initial discussions I had with the oncologists at Scottish Rite, so that inclusion came as a surprise, which I did not hesitate to voice. The radiation oncologist assured us that proper consultations with the oncologist from Scottish Rite would take place before the therapy began. That gave me some comfort.

The team ran through the process and all the side effects, from short- to long-term. Onsu was to have 15-20 sessions of radiation that would last less than three minutes each. It required her to stay still through the process, and if she couldn't, they would have to put her to sleep each time. I was certain she would lie still; after all, she could manage 45 minutes of an MIBG test without the help of any sedation, so I assured them she wouldn't need any help to stay still. 'That would be excellent,' was the cheery response we got from the medical personnel.

It was necessary to take measurements of the exact spots that would require radiation, given that the medical personnel have to go all out to ensure they protect the organs not affected or requiring exposure. To aid this, a cast had to be pre-ordered, as they would require it for shielding Onsu from the harmful ultraviolet rays. After all the explanations, I needed to sign a document to confirm they had briefed me; of course, paperwork was a part of hospital life, so we quickly got that out of the way.

Before we left the hospital that day, the radiation workers took measurements of Onsu's forehead and properly marked sections of her skin with a waterproof marker. Onsu was puzzled and asked me why the lady was writing on her body. I am certain she thought writing was reserved for the whiteboards and pieces of paper. The radiologist let out a warm chuckle and took time to explain why the writing was going on. They marked the abdominal region that aligned with Onsu's right adrenal gland, as well as a slight curve towards the spine. They took extra care around the spine to limit the exposure, as the radiation could affect her growth pattern.

Radiation started towards the end of December 2008, with the plan to finish by 23 January, 2009. Perfect timing, I thought. My estimated date of delivery was in the first week of February. With Onsu's pregnancy, I couldn't wait for her birth and hoped she would be born two weeks before the EDD. With this pregnancy, however, I hoped the two-week buffer before the EDD for having babies would elude me. I needed the baby to spend a few more weeks in my belly. It was tough enough managing one child with two hands, so having another child before wrapping up the radiation process would be almost impossible to manage alone.

The timing for the radiation was early; they expected us to arrive at the hospital between 6.30 and 7am daily. Day one of radiation was the trial run that would define whether or not Onsu would need sedation for future treatments. The process started with splendid news. The radiation oncologist informed us that there would be no radiation on her head, and I was ecstatic. The next step was to try out the radiation therapy without anaesthesia. Those were courageous steps Onsu took as she walked towards the radiation room. You would think she was a professional at it. Prior to that, I had worked on her psyche while promising her some irresistible treats if she stayed still for the procedure. She stepped in and got all ready, while I watched through a glass panel outside. Just when the medical personnel stepped out to start the process, my Miss Brave suddenly became nervous and let out a whimper that aborted the entire process, as precision was key. I don't think it disappointed me. I just realised it was a dream that had ended midway.

They promised to give her another chance the next day, but for day one, they required us to return to the preparation room. Anaesthesia it was! Time to sign papers again. I promptly gave the consent, and within seconds, she was in another world. Deep sleep had taken over, propofol at work. They rolled her into the therapy room and out again just as fast. It was really a quick one. It was now a waiting game for little Miss Sleepy to wake up, and when she did, the first thing she asked for was her treat. A deal was a deal.

Soon, we left for the Ronald McDonald House, our home away from home. We repeated the same routine the next day. She still could not stay still for the therapy, so we resolved propofol was the way forward. We made a friend there too, a pretty, eight-year-old girl who had a brain tumour. They always put both girls to sleep at about the same time, so naturally the mums got talking till the girls were rolled out again.

Our daily routine continued and was quite seamless. We knew the ropes now. In addition, we had begun the countdown to leaving the Ronald McDonald House, as we were moving into a new apartment. We were expecting my mum from Nigeria, having baby number two and so much more. With all the restrictions and the family growing, we had decided to rent a temporary-stay apartment on the same street where Tambu lived. The plan was to move in there right after the radiation therapy. I started exhibiting withdrawal symptoms because I now loved the Ronald McDonald House and the flexibility and freedom it gave me.

The consolation was that I was moving closer to family. I am not exactly sure of how I got to know about the property, but I remember that my brother and I had to inspect it the Saturday before I moved in, which coincidentally was the same day I expected my mum from Nigeria: 17 January, 2009. My brother discouraged Onsu and me from stopping by at his house because my nephew had pink eye and my daughter's immune system remained compromised. Well, we could not avoid it and had to stop by briefly. My nephew was not as boisterous, and I remember he stood on the chair, looking at me but not with the excitement he would usually have displayed. I did not read much into it because pink eye, or conjunctivitis, can be very uncomfortable. I recall having it sometime back and thought I had a grain of sand somewhere in my eyelids.

I returned to the Ronald McDonald House after inspecting and settling for the temporary house. Later that day, my mum arrived at Tambu's house. He brought her over to the Ronald McDonald House the next day, and, as expected, it thrilled us to see her. She spent the night with us, and we did a lot of catching up. Onsu requested that she joined us at the clinic the next day, which she was happy to do.

The next morning was Grandma's first peek into our routine, which we were almost done with anyway. We made it right on time to the hospital and walked in, with Onsu all cheery and ready to show off her grandma. She literally bounced into the hospital, all chitty-chatty. As soon as it was time for her propofol, her grandma witnessed the quick switch from exuberance to instant sleep and couldn't hold back her tears. It brought back memories of all I had dealt with. The road had been rocky indeed.

***

An old friend, Antai, had visited from London and coincidentally got to know I was in Atlanta. It had been about ten years or more since our paths crossed, so his offer to stop over at the Ronald McDonald House was welcome. He offered to drive us to the Mall of Georgia, as I had some last-minute shopping for the baby, who was due in less than two weeks. He kept his word and made it in good time to get us. My mum, Onsu and I hopped into the car and headed out.

The traffic was quite light, and we made it to the mall in less than an hour. We had just stepped inside when my phone rang. It was Tambu. The noise inside the mall made it difficult to hear him, so I made my way outside.

'Manyo, where are you?' he asked.

I said, 'I just got to Mall of Georgia'.

'Is Mummy with you?'

'Yes. What's up? Is everything okay?'

He choked back a sob. 'We lost Ata.'

'What?' Surely I hadn't heard him correctly.

'He is dead.'

'How?'

I just couldn't contain myself. I wailed. I cried and shouted. That was the last thing I expected to hear. *How can…? My favourite nephew gone? How?* Even now, shivers run down my spine when I remember that incident. It remains the worst thing that has happened to me.

We rushed off to their house, which was about 20 minutes away. It hurt so badly; I couldn't say anything coherent. That was 21 January, 2009. A day I will never forget. It really tested my faith yet again. I went to the funeral home, where Ata was peacefully sleeping. I prayed over him and trusted God for a miracle, for him to just get up, my every hope hinging on the Word of God.

I looked forward to hearing it was all a lie, that he was alive. I kept believing till we laid him to rest. Didn't I pray enough? The questions just will not end.

Rest on, darling Ata, till we meet again. You will always have an extra-special place in my heart.

***

On 23 January, 2009, we completed radiation therapy. Our stay at the Ronald McDonald House was now over and it was time to check out. A day we all should have been excited to celebrate, a huge milestone, ended in gloom and anxiety as our hearts were heavy.

The next phase of treatment was oral Accutane, a trade name for isotretinoin, which is considered an oral chemotherapy for many. It was a six-month course. We did not need to stay in the hospital. I needed a prescription, and monthly checks were required to ensure the drug was interacting well with Onsu's system and wasn't toxic to her vital organs.

On 29 January, six days after we left the Ronald McDonald House, I had an appointment with the gynaecologist. He carried out the routine urine tests, a scan, and in the process mentioned my cervix was slightly dilated. As was his usual practice, he performed a finger sweep of the cervix and said that when the labour pains became intense with some contractions, I should make my way straight to the hospital and check in.

Our reliable Aunty Ify was available to assist us. She had asked that I take my packed hospital bag with me while going for my antenatal checks, just in case the time was right. Though my carry-on was with me, I was certain I still had a couple of days to go, as my due date was in the first week of February. From the clinic, Aunty Ify and I went to Target Superstore to buy a few things. Barely two hours after the doctor's checks, the contractions started. It began mildly then got more intense. I did not want my water to break in a shop or mall as with my first pregnancy, so Aunty Ify rushed me to the hospital, assisted with the registration process and stayed on with me in the birthing room. We could not return home to get my mum and Onsu, so I reached out to the cab driver I frequently used, and he picked them up. Though I was in exceedingly great pain, I hoped my mum and Onsu would make it to the hospital before I had the baby. That did not happen. I gave birth before they arrived to our beautiful, adorable second daughter at precisely 4.32pm in Lawrenceville, Georgia.

I had searched for a name that best described the total experience of my pregnancy through to her birth, but all that kept coming to me was God's grace. I just didn't know how I pulled through. All I knew was that it was only by His grace. I had asked my dad for a name in my language, Ejagham, that could best describe God's grace. The closest we got after all the trials is her first name. So, our adorable, fair, full-haired daughter was named Onohnse Adomnyame Tamunoboma:

Onohnse: This in Ejagham means 'the goodness of God'.

Adomnyame: Directly translated as 'God's grace'. The Ghanaian names had come to stay to honour my children's heritage and their late grandfather.

Tamunoboma: A Kalabari name meaning 'God's grace still at work'.

Everything went smoothly, and Tambu came to the hospital the next day to take us back to our new apartment. We kept our gaze upwards.

***

Things were just not the same. It was strange. We should have been rejoicing, shouting, excited, but we were just quiet and in deep thoughts. Another celebration we could not quite have. Amidst thanksgiving, our hearts stayed weighed down. It was difficult to exist in that space without Ata.

A few days after we got home, the new big sister, Innomama Osunyameye Dickson, dressed in a light pink jumper, stared out into the woods behind the house for a while. I wasn't sure what the attraction was, but it was not a harmful act, so

I paid little attention to her. Shortly afterwards, she turned around with an enormous smile, and the next thing I heard took me by surprise.

'Mummy, I saw Ata.'

That stopped me right in my tracks. 'What?' I asked.

'I saw Ata. He says he is happy.'

It dazed me to get that message from a child so young, but I was certain it was not a mistake. He was in a good place. That gave me some peace, and I only wished he could appear to his grieving parents to help them with some closure too.

***

I had long planned for my mum's 60th birthday and how she would be celebrated. She had been a source of strength. Life had dealt her fresh blows yet again, but she kept standing strong and being extremely positive. She was my ever-present lamentation pillow, but her favourite phrase that helped reshape my thinking and attitude about life was, 'It could have been worse'. Her positivity rubbed off on me over time, as she continually tried to get me to see the brighter side of life. So, if you know me personally and think I am overly positive, I owe more of that to her. Well, here it was, 8 March, 2009, and I realised yet again that man can but only plan. Mum was 60, and we had barely just laid her grandson to rest. We made some food and took pictures to mark the day. Thankfully, Tambu invited us for a programme in the Presbyterian church where he worshipped. We still owed all allegiance to God.

We continued to take it one day at a time. Onsu's medical checks continued to go well. She tolerated Accutane well enough. My mum's stay was scheduled to end in April when Tobin returned to the US, possibly for the last shift before we returned to Nigeria. The baton was exchanged between my husband and mum; the last lap began. Tobin could finally see his second daughter, Onohnse, who he nicknamed 'Nana'.

***

It was time to reset and pack up. I had been out of Nigeria and the office for almost 11 months straight, the longest I had been away. New anxieties, adjustments, expectations, realities. Of course, we wished we could stay longer, especially since I had to return to the US with Osunyameye every three months for her medical check-ups, but we did what we had to do to keep moving forward.

On Saturday, 2 May, 2009, we returned to Port Harcourt. Emotions ran wild, memories rushed right back, but then gratitude welled up within us. As we stepped into the house, some lovely family and friends were right there with meals and a cake to ensure we settled in okay. The first thing Tobin did was to say a prayer of gratitude. It was a day of great joy. The next day, we arrived at the King's Assembly in Port Harcourt, where we worshipped as a family, to have Onohnse dedicated to God and to use the golden opportunity to thank God before the congregation for His mercies and faithfulness through the journey.

Hilda Manyo Dickson

The day after the dedication, I returned to work. It was time to restart the engine and forge ahead. It felt strange fitting into the workspace again, though I was excited to be back. There again, at lunchtime, my caring colleagues and friends arranged a surprise welcome back get-together for me with some bosses in attendance. How thoughtful that was! It was wonderful to be back.

Settling in had its daunting parts. My first day at work is one that would not be forgotten in a hurry. Getting to work was straightforward; it took me about 30 minutes. I dropped Onohnse off at the office crèche. She coped well and barely cried, from what I gathered. We left the office at 4pm, and I was certain we would be home before five. Little did I know I was in for an adventure. Apparently, the roads were in a horrible state, and some minor works were going on here and there. With a three-month-old baby in the car, the last thing I wanted was an extended travel time. We spent three hours in traffic, with the baby wailing from hunger. It was a wake-up call. Moving out of that vicinity was a necessity if I had to juggle everything and remain sane.

***

Three months later, Osunyameye and I returned to Children's Healthcare of Atlanta for a follow-up check. I think it was at that point that everything we had been through dawned on me. Anxiety started building up again. Over that week Onsu had to have the MIBG, CT scan, ECG, blood tests and more. What would the results say? Would we be able to return to Nigeria within a week? I had, after all, left a six-month-old baby back at home. I immediately took hold of myself and shook it off, as it appeared fear was beginning to creep in. It was obvious I had heard too many stories about cancer and sudden relapses.

Thankfully, the medical checks went well, and I was extremely grateful to the Almighty Father. Our family would be reunited, and my daughters would continue to grow in good health.

CHAPTER THIRTEEN

Yet Another Unplanned Bouquet

Getting pregnant had been an issue from the onset, so I'd never been fussy about being on birth control. Moreover, breastfeeding acts as a birth control, or at least that is what some studies infer. So, it wasn't until January 2010, when Onohnse turned one year old, that I thought it right to begin the search for a contraceptive. Several things led to that decision. Early in our marriage, my husband had expressed his desire to have two children, while I desired three. This happened even before we realised we would have to wait almost five years to have the first child. Over the years, I became even more convinced two was the perfect number after the journey with a sick child and the discoveries in the process. Before marriage, genetic testing for genotypes was recommended by the church we worshipped. The genotype represents our exact genetic makeup, and a wrong combination could lead to having children with sickle cell anaemia, which could be fatal in bad cases.

Our test showed my genotype was AA and my husband's AS. There had been a previous result that came up during a pre-employment test that showed I was AS. I assumed it was a diagnostic error, as I had always known AA as my genotype, even when I took ill in the university and did the genotype confirmatory test. After Onsu took ill, I ran a second confirmatory test in the US to be certain there were no errors. In addition, I was pregnant at the time and already dealing with a sick child, so I really did not want to add sickle cell to the mix. The results came out shortly afterwards, and they confirmed my genotype was AS. I was devastated, not because there was anything wrong with AS genotype as a stand-alone, but the combination for a couple was a no-no! The decision to use a contraceptive made perfect sense.

I stepped into the doctor's office, not even sure of what to expect, as this was the first time I considered using a contraceptive. I chuckled at the thought that the same lady who had waited for years for a baby was now about to put a stop to the childbearing activities. The irony of life. After all the pleasantries and enquiry on why I was there, the next questions and steps from the doctor got me recalculating.

'When was your last period?'

'I'm not sure, sir. I need to calculate it, but I think it is late', I responded.

'Well, if it was not in the last week, then wait for your period and return for the contraceptive when next it shows up.'

'Doctor, don't you have a way of checking and inserting the coil rather than the torture of waiting for the period?'

'No' was his firm and simple answer.

I left the clinic with a feeling of defeat. I did a quick calculation and realised I had missed my period. I usually had a perfect cycle. I started waiting and, in the process, took a pregnancy test. As you might surmise, I was pregnant! If there is anything like instant depression, that's what I went into. It was so difficult to comprehend. Many thoughts held me bound. *What if the child has sickle cell anaemia? How will I forgive myself? When will my story line slow down? How will my employers perceive it? Was I careless? Will this cause a strain in my marriage?* The questions were just unending. The only things that held me from seeking medical termination was my belief in God and my value system. It was definitely a mind game. My faith was being tested yet again.

I was not myself for almost three months. Luckily, before it became too late, I scheduled a meeting to see our pastor after a midweek service. As I walked into his office I chuckled, trying to be my usual jovial self.

'Good evening, Pastor,' I said.

'Good evening, Hilda. How are you?'

'Pastor, I have sinned.'

'You have fallen out of grace?'

'No! Oh Pastor, not that type of sin.'

I paused.

'I am pregnant.'

Looking surprised and laughing at the same time, he said, 'Oh, congratulations!'

While still in the discussion, his wife, Mrs. Yemisi Ugoh, whom I consider a close friend, stepped into the office briefly. When I mentioned why I was feeling low, she started laughing and congratulating me. She even joked that she wished she was the one with such great news. I smiled and continued my counselling session.

'Pastor, you know I was done with my two girls. You also know this genotype issue. It has not been funny.'

'Hildaaaa, where is your faith? You know God has always shown up for you when you believe.'

He took time to counsel me and pray with me.

That reminder was a turning point for me. I was able to activate my support system intentionally and took the required steps to return to the Giver of Life. There was a shift, and I got my groove back. I displaced fear with faith yet again and was ready to trust God for a miracle.

When I was about five months gone, I had yet another scare. This time, it was a lump on my left breast. I had it excised during a trip I made in May 2010 for Onsu's medical check-ups. The pregnancy went well from then onwards. I focused on work and my deliverables till I had to leave to the United States shortly after Onsu's fourth birthday in September.

Hilda Manyo Dickson

***

On 15 October 2010, my sister-in-law Ada took me to the clinic to see my gynaecologist. He checked my cervix and, as before, asked that I return to the hospital immediately once contractions began. I expected my husband and daughters to arrive that evening from Nigeria, so Ada took me to an Asian store nearby to get the items I needed to fix a meal for the family. While shopping, yet again, intense contractions kicked in. Ada drove me to the same hospital where I had given birth to my two girls, but this time I was bent on having an epidural— life just had to be easier.

They rolled me into a room to check my vitals and other parameters. My cervix was already dilated to 2cm. Before the nurses could set up for an epidural, I was fully dilated and was wheeled into the birthing room. My doctor was contacted as soon as I arrived at the hospital, but before he could arrive, the midwives present had delivered me of a son. The doctor made it in time to clean me up. The birthing process happened within 40 minutes of my arrival at the hospital, which made the nurses nickname me 'Little Miss Quickie'. Like his siblings, this baby's names reflect the seasons and the times in which he was born:

Osakibiteim: God's time is best

Nyamekye: God's gift

God is humorous and continues to surprise us with exceptional gifts even during the greatest challenges. Osaki is a vibrant young man with a mind of his own and is the spitting image of his dad.

After a diagnosis that declared it would be impossible to have children naturally, we now have two daughters and a son, all naturally conceived.

He blesses amid challenges.

EPILOGUE

The journey through life can sometimes be more of an unintended adventure, filled with contingencies, abrupt reversals, and multiple surprises. As I pause to ponder daily, several questions spring up from within: What is the very essence of life? How do we choose to live out our lives? With what purposes, partners, preparation and commitments do we travel the long road to find fulfilment? The story of every expedition is invariably underscored by one or more themes, those fundamental principles from which we may draw lessons and gain values. An expression that wraps it all for me is this: Live life knowing that the countdown to the answer is always on.

In the following pages, I recap the lessons and coping mechanisms I have gained along my journey, the tools and weapons I forged that equipped me, treasures I found that enriched me, all of which I strongly believe could be helpful for readers who wish to lean in. The purpose is to impress the minds of others with the principles, ideals and truths that furthered my life, that they too may find strength, encouragement, hope and direction for their own journeys.

FACING TRIALS

One verse from the Bible is on a constant replay mode in my mind: 'Count it all joy when you fall into various trials knowing that the testing of your faith produces patience' (James 1:2-3).

Some scriptures are difficult to chew on. Counting joy during trials? How does that work? It sounds more like being happy for pain—a concept I struggle with, and I bet you do too. I know good comes out of bad, just as growth is borne out of pain, but focus and the right attitude remain important keys. Patience is a key requirement for everyone, especially when it is so obvious you can do nothing on your own. Furthermore, our inner strength is derived and sustained from being totally dependent on a higher power and not at the mercy of whatever situation you find yourself. With this at the back of my mind, I like to think this scripture means that I am responsible for my reaction in any circumstance I find myself in. I can choose to moan about what has befallen me, tell myself it could have been worse or just hinge my faith on God's promises.

WORD INFUSION, A VITAL INGREDIENT

There is another Bible verse that keeps echoing within me: 'For out of the abundance of the heart, the mouth speaks' (Luke 6:45b).

There must be an outpouring from the heart when issues or pain points get triggered. What is in your heart? How much have you internalised? How has your relationship been with the only wise God? How have you nurtured that relationship? Do you have enough arrows? I ask because you cannot give what you do not have.

When the road is smooth, it's important to always stay in the place of communion with the Father, because when the rough waves show up you realise that there's really no one to turn to but the Supreme Being. I had gone through a couple of trials and challenges right from the days of my youth. I had grown, matured, become better, but nothing prepared me for what I had ahead of me as much as the God-partnership and spiritual network I had built during my journey. Even before my daughter's diagnosis, I was in disarray.

I could only liken it to groping in the dark, as I had no clue what was going on. We roamed from one hospital to another and still ended up with wrong or inconclusive diagnoses. The string that held us together was the infused Word of God and the connection built with Him before the trial reared its ugly head. Prayers and positive confessions based on what we had personalised were the go-to tools.

When we finally knew what the problem was and the journey progressed, I searched for messages of hope or any positive news that did not pronounce neuroblastoma a death sentence, but it was so hard to find any. I could not find anyone selling success stories, and no one was sharing coping mechanisms. The medical team had so much to offer on positive or negative prognoses, how to manage a child dealing with cancer, and much more. But beyond the medical team, where were the believers? I needed real-life experiences of people who walked or were walking the same road. I needed faith-filled and inspiring articles on conquering the monster called cancer.

BE OPEN

Two simple words that need courage to embrace: be open. Isaiah 55:8 says, 'For my thoughts are not your thoughts neither are your ways my ways, declares the Lord'. Most times we pray and follow it through by limiting God. We define our expectations so much that when the answers come through, we are still looking for them. I never imagined my life partner would be a colleague; nor did I ever imagine our connection would spring from the death of a friend. In the openness and friendship, things unfolded, took a unique twist, and God turned it around in a way I least expected. We need to be deliberate in praying for the spirit of discernment such that we do not miss out on His plans for us.

TRUST COMPLETELY

According to my favourite scripture, Proverbs 3:5-6, 'Trust in the Lord with all your heart and lean not on your own understanding. In all your ways acknowledge Him and He will direct your paths.' There were so many lessons in different phases of my life that made it easier to trust God completely in tougher circumstances. I found myself vulnerable to God, like a young child looks up to an earthly father, believing he is a superhero. I could almost touch God in every situation I encountered.

When I accepted a commitment ring from Tobin, one reason for waiting beyond the programme he enrolled for was for my husband to get a job. When the job did not come through, I was neither in a hurry to get married, nor was I under any pressure. Tobin felt differently. He believed we needed to move on. I only became convinced when I prayed and had peace. When we took a trip to visit my folks, no one asked where my husband-to-be worked or what line of business he was in. I marvelled and asked my dad why he had not bothered to ask what Tobin did for a living. He simply said, 'I see prospects and not the present'. That was profound for me. When you trust, you don't wait for the complete picture or puzzle; you trust God, who sees the end from the beginning.

Tobin had a good saving habit he formed when he was a kid. Which again reminds me of the scripture Proverbs 22:6: 'Train a child in the way he should go; even when he is old, he will not depart from it'. He had funds set aside for the wedding, which he saved from his earlier jobs. I had savings too, but surprisingly, we had all the funds fully intact even after the wedding. We enjoyed tremendous goodwill from family and friends, leading to a beautiful fairytale wedding, which I strongly believe is linked to the fact that we trusted God completely. We prepared our five loaves and two fishes, and God took charge and multiplied.

My choice to have National Youth Service Corps in Port Harcourt was mainly driven by the desire to work in an oil company. That did not work out as planned. I ended up with a bank. It appeared I was not cut out for the petroleum industry, because a few opportunities had disappointingly slipped by, yet just a casual stroll across the road to see a friend brought about another opportunity. It was late, the company had stopped collecting applications going by the advert, but I persisted and played my part by sending in the application. Through the process, I had to trust God completely. I was not more deserving of the job or even more intelligent, but I am reminded of Romans 9:15: 'I will have mercy on whom I will have mercy and I will have compassion on whom I will have compassion'. Persistence and faith were mine to exhibit; completion was God's.

STAY VIGILANT

I just had a breakthrough! Finally, the enemy can let me breathe, or at least that was my expectation.

Well, while still basking in the euphoria of being pregnant and making plans on how the baby would have a comfortable SUV to ride in, I was reminded of yet another Bible verse, 1 Peter 5:8, that reads, 'Be sober, be vigilant; because your adversary the devil walks about like a roaring lion seeking whom he may devour'. How else would I explain the fall that led to the bleeding episode I had just before the twelfth week of my pregnancy, or the armed robbers snatching the car we just bought? Earthly possessions did not matter when I saw the gun pointed at my husband. All I pleaded was for Tobin's life to be spared.

Onsu's birth was an act of God's mercy, His gift to us for our trust and faith in Him. With such a lovely child, what else could we wish for? The first 18 months compensated for the wait. We dedicated Osunyameye to God, met the exclusive breastfeeding goal of six months, cooked most of her meals from scratch, and believed she was in good shape and then boom! An unexplainable sickness struck, and the confusion, doubts, concerns, anxieties, fear and other negative emotions rushed in. But then we were reminded that even roses have thorns. We must be vigilant. Never let down your guard, and keep your reservoir full of God's Word and promises. You will need to draw from it when the enemy strikes.

GUARD YOUR HEART: REFUSE TO ENTERTAIN FEAR

The enemy thrives on instilling fear in us, but our currency as Christ's followers is faith. 2 Timothy 1:7 says, 'For God has not given us a spirit of fear, but of power and of love and of a sound mind'. I refer yet again to the recommendation by another parent that I join a virtual support group on neuroblastoma. I did, but it messed up my mind and only caused me nightmares. The stories of relapse or death featured in the group much more than the positive news I eagerly desired. That website was the main trigger and partial origin of this book. I vowed to document my journey and share some good news when God took us through the process and gave us victory. It has taken so long to put this together, and I have dealt with guilt pangs, no doubt. However, I am grateful for an opportunity to share my story and my support systems during the tough times, hoping that it banishes fear and at least one person will be encouraged or dare to believe that actual healing is possible.

So, it was important for me to guard my heart when obstacles showed up, because several views would emerge, some good, some doom and gloom. If you have so-called prophets around you, it could aggravate your fear level, depending on which angle the 'prophecy' is coming from. Proverbs 4:23 has this to say: 'Guard your heart with all diligence, for out of it springs the issues of life'. Did I entertain fear sometimes? Most definitely I did! I am only human. At those times, the only choice I had was to step up my faith level and keep my trust in God. Was it easy? No! I just refused to stay in the place of fear and kept moving to find a solution, while not relenting on seeking God's face.

My comforting scripture in time of crisis is Deuteronomy 31:6: 'Be strong and of good courage, do not fear nor be afraid of them for the Lord your God, He it is who goes with you. He will not leave you nor forsake you'.

NOURISHING YOUR MIND

When the diagnosis remained unclear, we had to travel out of Nigeria and away from everything familiar. I needed to feed my mind with good stuff – listen to messages, worship songs, just stay in God's presence somehow. A friend, Eruvy, had given me her portable CD player to travel with. The compact disc she had inside had a very reassuring song which was coined from Jeremiah 32:17: 'Ah Lord God, thou hast made the heavens and the earth by thy great power. Nothing is too difficult for thee'.

The lyrics of the song were like a continuous refrain of this Bible verse. I played this song repeatedly till it became real to me. It always made me break out in worship and tears. I played it even more when the diagnosis came through. I got charged up, and it strengthened me. Though I did not intentionally keep a journal of all the times God showed up for me or us (which, by the way, is very important), as I sang each time I was reminded of the great and mighty things God had done in the past, and gratitude welled up within me.

Then I referred to Proverbs 10:22 that states: 'The blessing of the Lord makes one rich and He adds no sorrow with it'. That energised me and reminded me that God's Word is His bond … though it doesn't always play out the way we expect it to.

THE POWER OF THE SPOKEN WORD

Words hold power. There is a releasing quality in every word, which, like everything created in this world, fulfills a purpose. Proverbs 18:21 has this to say: 'Life and death are in the power of the tongue, and those who love it will eat its fruit'. Our words, therefore, give our lives direction; they shape our destinies on earth.

Let's rewind some months before Osunyameye's birth. There I was, miraculously pregnant, when barely three months before the doctor had proclaimed boldly, 'It is impossible for you to conceive a baby naturally'. Thankfully, at the time, I was quick to confess my faith and speak the words taken from Exodus 23:26: 'There shall be none barren in the land, neither male nor female'. Speaking these words helped me release and anchor the power of my faith.

Consciously or otherwise, we magnify our problems and glorify the enemy when we remain silent, quietly accept and even repeat negative statements and proclamations over our lives. No!

Magnify God! His greatness is comparable to nothing I can imagine. He specialises in impossibilities. Speak out His Word and promises over your life. The power of such proclaimed spirit-filled words reverberates to you and is re-absorbed by your soul.

THE POWER IN A NAME

Following closely from the spoken word are the names we are called daily.

After Osunyameye was born, the choice of her name was deliberate. It embodied the boundless and miraculous power of God which we experienced through her birth.

'There is power in a name' is a quote we hear so often. When Osunyameye took ill, it was clear yet again that her name was not accidental. The name was also her destiny. I had to activate the might in the name and that of the spoken word by requesting that everyone called her Onsu. As it was called, it never ceased to remind me that nothing is impossible with God.

I remember one of the senior doctors walking into the hospital room and challenging my faith.

'What is this thing I hear about asking that your daughter be called some name or something – Onsu – other than her first name?'

I explained to him, 'Onsu is a short form of Osunyameye, which is her middle name. It means, "With God nothing is impossible".' I enlightened him about my belief that each time we called her name it was a prophecy over her life that revalidated my expectation of a miraculous healing for her.

With a fling of his hand, he said, 'That's for those who believe such things'.

He didn't hesitate to give me the news of a poor prognosis and how difficult it was to have anything fixed to say about neuroblastoma, since it is aggressive. I thanked him for dropping by and reminded him of the greatness of the God I serve. I was not about to magnify the problem. So yes, your faith will always be challenged, but it does not negate the power in the word.

TURN ON THE RIGHT ATTITUDE, ACT IN FAITH

I was in an unfamiliar environment – the hospital. Other than childbirth, I had been an outpatient all my life, but here I was, spending one to two weeks of each month in the hospital and the rest of the month managing hospital visits. There is always someone in a better or worse place than you are. Some pathetic cases brought tears to my eyes and reminded me to give thanks.

I was surrounded by many people willing to provide support. I needed a network, no doubt, but I had to choose carefully. I smiled a lot, exuding so much cheer that I became a topic of discussion around the hospital corridors. A parent once approached me to state how my smile gave her hope. She asked how I stayed cheerful, though I did not have my family in Atlanta. I mentioned my brother and his family lived there, though I knew she was referring to my husband.

I thought that was all until another parent, whose child had the same diagnosis and with whom I'd struck a chord, stepped right into our room. She said, 'Hey, Hilda, I hear you're Hindu, and that's why you smile a lot and manage the treatment so well. Is that true?' I laughed really hard. I asked her to join me in watching a programme that was showing on the TV at that time. It was Oral Roberts ministries, *The Place for Miracles*. I asked her if it looked like a Hindu programme. I seized the opportunity to share the source of my strength with her. I clarified that I was a follower of Christ. I did not smile because it was easy; I smiled because I was acting. I had come to the point where I knew I could do nothing on my own and had no power to change the situation. So yes, believe. Then act like it till you get it.

I had to trust God. I had to activate my faith in God. I had to act till I could have the desired miracle. That is why I tuned in to Oral Roberts ministry's programme regularly. Different people shared testimonies and miracles each night that showed a touch from God. Beyond reading the Bible, I watched programmes that could build my faith and tackle any form of fear. God is no respecter of persons. If He could do it for others, and for me, then He surely will do it for you. I remember telling the mum that came to my room that carrying the problem on my forehead would not bring about a solution or even ease any pain. I needed the right attitude, and the choice was mine. Your strength and faith will rub off on others. Don't be discouraged. God's grace remains enough for us.

SURRENDER ALL YOUR AFFAIRS TO GOD

Let us step a bit into the past. Recall that at the time my husband asked me to marry him, I took some time off to pray and wait on the Lord for direction. I did not want to be carried away by his looks or any butterfly feelings, as many would describe it.

I just needed to be sure I had clarity and was at peace. Right after the period of prayer and fasting, I did a medical test to be sure that all parameters were fine. My genotype was, of course, a key index I had to check. Well, fast-forward into the future, and further checks after the marriage confirmed my genotype to be AS (same as my husband) and not AA, as I had been led to believe before marriage. What was I to do at the time? Get angry? Take a walk? I sure could have chosen any of the wrong actions, but because I was certain there were no games involved as I had sought God prior to this time, I stayed put. If I approached God and He gave me the required peace to step out, then who am I?

Isaiah 26:3 lets us know that, 'You keep him in Perfect Peace whose mind is stayed on You because he trusts in You'.

Today, we are blessed with two daughters who are AS. And the son I almost didn't have because of fear, is the only one with the AA genotype. This is not to encourage anyone to dabble into mismatched genotype marriages; I did not. It is all in my miracle basket which I refer to and draw strength from. So, I ask again, who are you partnering with or who are you in a covenant with?

STAYING STRONG

Was the journey overwhelming? Yes, it certainly was. Were there nights I cried? Yes, a lot of nights. I even did some crying during the day. The only promise I made to myself was to make sure my daughter did not see my tears. I needed to be strong for her; I needed to see her smile through the pain; I needed her to see and feel hope. At times, I would cry my heart out while she slept. It could be very therapeutic, especially if one is not crying from the point of hopelessness and self-pity.

At other times, I was so fatigued from all the throwing up, cleaning up after her, the pain she dealt with, the pregnancy stress and sleepless nights, that even prayer eluded me. I would play some music to the point that crying set in naturally. Strangely, I never asked, 'Why me?' as I could not wish it on an enemy. I only asked that God show forth with His healing power. Of course, I could not just keep crying, so there had to be other ways of coping.

The time difference between Nigeria and the US made it a bit difficult to get through to our pastor at some points. I knew he was praying; the church was praying, and even the labour unions at work were praying, but there were times I just needed to share with someone and have them hold me up in prayers. So yes, I had some 24-hour prayer lines I could call anytime, even if all of America was asleep. They were always ready and willing to listen, pray and encourage me.

Some nights were turbulent. I watched my daughter groaning, and I could do nothing to soothe her. All I could do was to draw strength and endurance from the bank of the heart, from an inner wealth that had already been created there through previously depositing uplifting truths and enriching my space with helpful spiritual knowledge. Remember, therefore, to consistently feed your soul with an abundance of good and positive thoughts, as these will one day serve to fortify and encourage you in your hour of need.

THE VALUE OF RELATIONSHIPS

We worshipped at Victory World Church Norcross each time we were out of the hospital. It was necessary to keep feeding the spirit. I recall walking up to Pastor Dennis Rouse to agree with us in prayer before the transplant, and a few other programmes I attended to keep the positive attitude intact. Beyond the helplines and churches, there was the body of Christ in human form – friends, family, bosses, church members, who constantly called from different parts of the world. You need relationships. Don't wait for problems before reaching out to people; just go on and build your networks. You never know when they will be required. Don't make friends only in time of trouble, as that could become parasitic. Make friends for what you have to offer. Make intentional, positive deposits into your relationships. The same way you deposit or invest money in financial institutions and eventually withdraw is exactly what I expect of relationships. None of us can exist in total isolation. We all need people. There was so much help and love, even from the medical personnel.

Before the end of my stay, some friends took steps to visit me in the United States. Amara, my boss-turned-friend and sister, visited from Paris. Chioma, another friend-turned-sister, visited with her six-month-old baby from Nigeria via Seattle. My sisters-in-law Onsu Snr and Singto visited at different times. Singto made the last set of braids I had on in 2008, before I cut my hair in solidarity with my daughter who lost hers from cancer treatments. Onsu Snr returned when I lost my nephew to ensure she attended the funeral service. The kind gestures were unending. Many people sent me money and clothes. I had so many friends that had turned into sisters. Nkechi N-J ordered maternity clothes straight to me, and Nkechi N sent funds across. Ivana and Onome, my colleagues at work, sent some funds and so did my team at work. Oke, who I met at church, parted with what we considered an enormous sum for a casual friendship. Chichi of KC Healthcare showed up with flowers, food items and loads of cheer. Aunty Ify launched me into driving in the US by giving me a car after Onsu's transplant, which I used till I left for Nigeria in May. Or was it my siblings, my mum or bosses who stuck their necks out? Or Mrs. Ofili-Okonkwo who hand-carried my case file when there was no policy to cater for a parent who was away from work for so long with a child, just to ensure I returned to a job? I could go on and on. Several people were an extension of God's hands through the trials. Help was constantly available. There is a declaration our pastor makes over the congregation weekly that encapsulates the need for people or networks. He says, 'Men and women are divinely motivated and are using their position, influence and resources to assist you now'.

God will always use our fellow men to assist us. People matter to God, so they should matter to you and me. Value them. Have the right set of people in your travel party, and surround yourself with the right support system. We all need each other.

FEEDING THE FLAME OF HOPE

Staying expectant and always anticipating positive outcomes are things that should never be underestimated. They are hope builders. This is relatable to having faith, but beyond that, the actions matter. I could liken it to keeping a testimony journal. What comes to mind readily are the two programmes that were being run for cancer patients by different non-profit organisations. One was Flashes of Hope, which set out to create lifetime memories for children dealing with cancer. The idea was one of smiling through pain. They offered professional photographs at no cost to patients or families, so we all worked hard at smiling or putting our best face on. Many of us looked forward to having a session with them each time there was an opportunity. There was a natural joy that came with expecting them. I look at those pictures today and remain convinced about the faithfulness of God.

The other programme, which I found equally intriguing, was the Beads of Courage. Their mission was to provide the Innovative Arts in Medicine programme for children coping with serious illnesses. I remember the first time they handed my daughter a string and beads. Every bead was a symbol of an event or experience. They stood for poking, platelet or red blood cell transfusions, a medical check-up, a biopsy, a bumpy journey... the possibilities went on and on. It started off with beads that clearly spelled out the patient's name, and it grew from there, with five yellow beads for each day of chemotherapy, white beads for pokes, if I remember well, to bigger beads for milestones or really bumpy hurdles and so on. Onsu looked forward to collecting beads each time till she had a really long, multicoloured neck ornament. Each bead honoured courage. I learned a lot through helping her string the beads into the necklace. It reminded me of the faithfulness of God. It was a virtual journey of all the rough patches God had taken us through and a reminder that we were still standing.

I could liken this to the attitude while waiting for God's manifestation, step by step. I remained focused, expectant and thankful, irrespective of the storm raging around me. It is important to keep expecting a positive outcome and to remain gratefully mindful of and encouraged by the triumphs over previous difficult challenges. Thanks to the non-profit organisations that assisted in keeping our eyes on the ultimate goal by cheering us up each step of the way.

THE LAW OF GIVING

The Bible encourages us to give cheerfully. 2 Corinthians 9:7 states: 'Each of you should give what you have decided in your heart to give, not reluctantly or under compulsion, for God loves a cheerful giver'. Beyond being on the receiving side, give! I learned long ago that you cannot outgive God.

For each change I have sought in my adult life, I initiated an element of giving. When I needed to decide on which job to settle for after my National Youth Service Corps, I had a seven-point prayer request. I made a pledge by faith. I did not have money at the time but was bent on using my meagre monthly stipend for a six-month period to redeem it. I assigned 50 percent of the funds to an orphanage and the other 50 percent to the church. Unexpectedly, within a month of making that pledge, I received some funds from clothes I sent to America for sale two years earlier. I had forgotten about the outfits and already considered it a terrible deal. I was quick to obey and moved to redeem my pledge by visiting the orphanage with food items and remitting funds to the church.

I dare say God met every prayer point on the list in quick succession. When I wanted to change jobs to something better, I increased my giving too. I gave security guards and other low-income earners tangible sums and not just the loose change in my purse. While waiting for a child, I kept giving. When she was sick, I never stopped giving. I systematically increase my offering depending on the shift I expect.

Seek opportunities to give towards helping people in need and growing the kingdom's agenda. The rewards are huge, I can testify. Different people have different ideologies about tithing. Giving is not all about money or tithing; it's your time, your talent, your resources, your listening ear, your presence, patience, encouragement, moral support and understanding. You should give to others with your being and nature. It is not about throwing resources around or funding other people's habits.

Just give wisely and be that shoulder someone can lean on.

THE POWER AND ALL-IMPORTANCE OF PRAYER

Even after the victory, I cannot overemphasise this constant. James 5:14 admonishes that, 'Is anyone among you sick? Let him call for the elders of the church and let them pray over him, anointing him with oil in the name of the Lord'.

Prayers move the hands that rule the world. I never left for a medical check-up without our dear Pastor Chris Ugoh putting my husband and I on a prayer/fasting programme and capping it up by praying for Onsu and anointing her. We started off going for the follow-up checks with a lot of fear. The devil always reminded us of the possibility of a relapse, poor prognosis and the like. The prayer sessions with Pastor Chris helped a lot. Prayer not only builds your faith and trust in God, as well as your spiritual strength, but it dispels fear and fills you with inner peace and calmness, enabling you to live a life free of worry and full of adventure. Over time, following this course, we spoke to ourselves and, as a family, converted medical visits to memorable vacations by adding an adventure to it. We consolidated our prayers with activity, deliberately going to recreation and adventure parks prior to the checks to keep our spirits high and positive. Here is a short poem that pretty much sums it up:

'Blest is he whose heart always
Deep in God confides;
Who within His love and Grace
Gratefully abides'.

CLOSING WORDS

Challenges come and keep coming. Mine have not stopped. This is just a portion of my life's journey. The enemy's goal is to destabilise you. 'Your adversary the devil prowls about like a roaring lion seeking whom to devour' (1 Peter 5:8). Every challenge that appears to have a mission to sink you is a propelling force towards a greater outcome. I choose to refer to challenges as temporary discomfort, knowing that pain leads to growth, and you move forward because of pain points. And when you have the assurance of scripture that all things are working for your good, or that what the enemy meant for evil, God will use for your good, you should rest easy!

The road to fulfilment and victory often requires effort and self-exertion, but rest assured you are empowered to overcome every obstacle in your path if you partner with the Sovereign God. He does not go back on His promises. He promised never to leave or forsake us, and that remains true.

OSUNYAMEYE encapsulated the journey of my life thus far, as I have truly witnessed the words of Luke 1:37: 'For with God nothing will be impossible'. What is that negative news, diagnosis or situation you think is impossible? Are you ready to defy the words of men? Then think,

Osunyameye. The Impossibility Specialist is always at work to turn the situation in your favour.

It is with that awareness that I encourage you to continue pushing, recalling that if you faint in the day of adversity, then your strength is small. Don't be weighed down by what you see on your way. Stay focused on the goal and be spurred to continuously forge ahead, knowing that faith that has not been tested cannot be trusted.

The fire will not consume you!

The trip to US in March 2008 before the diagnosis.

Innomama lost her personality September 2008

Innomama with her aunty...a break
from the hospital.

Innomama and Dad on one of the
hospital visits.

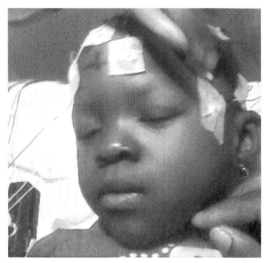

Electroencephalogram (EEG) on
Innomama's 2nd birthday.

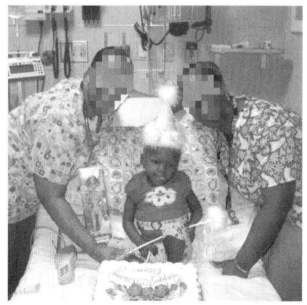

Innomama's 2nd birthday in CHOA.

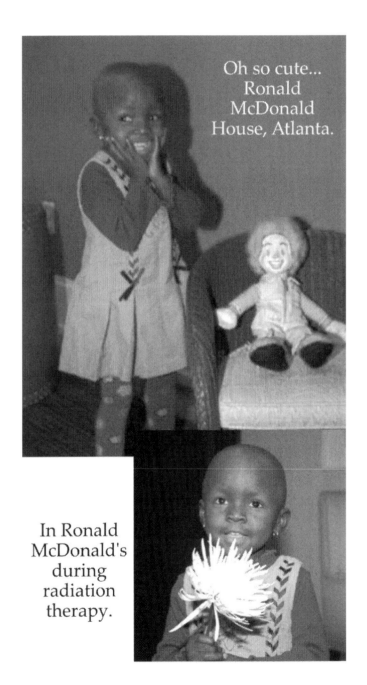

Oh so cute...
Ronald
McDonald
House, Atlanta.

In Ronald
McDonald's
during
radiation
therapy.

Home with my new born and her
doctor, Innomama.

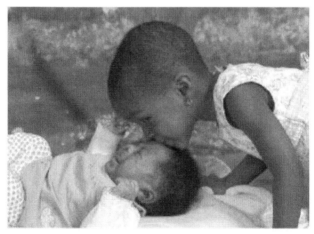

Innomama post treament with
Onohnse at six weeks -
March 8th, 2009.

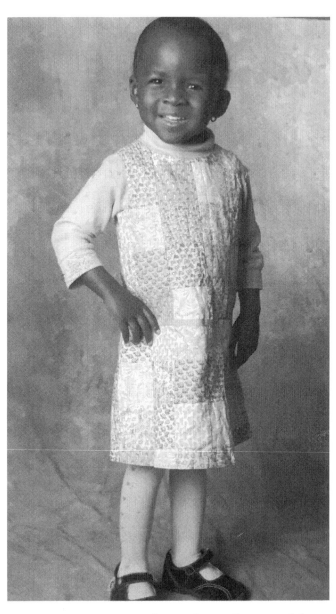

Innomama, ready to face the world.

Three
generations;
Grandma at 60.

The whole family in April 2021...
Faithful God.

ABOUT THE AUTHOR

HILDA MANYO DICKSON is a finance professional of over two decades, a John Maxwell certified speaker and coach. She is passionate about financial management and harnesses her experience as a chartered accountant to educate other women about their finances and help them multiply their streams of income.

While living through unimaginable personal challenges of her own, she was inspired to write about her experience in order to help others stay hopeful amid their storms. To those who know and love her, she is the 'Encourager', a friend who is committed to helping those around her maintain a positive outlook, no matter what they are passing through.

Her faith in God, love for family, and fitness fuels Hilda in her daily life. Wife to a fine, pragmatic man and mother to three gorgeous children, she loves good company, cooking, travelling, shopping, writing and listening to exhilarating music.

To connect:
Email: glidewithhmd@gmail.com
Website: glidewithhmd.com
Facebook: Hilda Manyo Dickson
LinkedIn: Hilda Manyo Dickson

Notes

Osunyameye

Notes

Nothing is Impossible with God

Printed in Great Britain
by Amazon

69332205R00161